# FROM
# GLORY
# TO
# GLORY

## A 52 WEEK DEVOTIONAL

### BY JEREMY AND SARAH PEARSONS

# FROM GLORY TO GLORY

© 2018 Pearsons Ministries International

Printed in the United States of America.

ISBN: 978-1-7325091-0-8

We dedicate this book to the partners of
Pearsons Ministries International.


Partners, God has been entirely faithful to us, and He's done it through you. We love you, and we pray for you every day. We say, "Be blessed. Be increased. Advance, rise up, and may the goodness of the Lord be seen in your life."

Him we preach,

Jeremy and Sarah

# TABLE OF CONTENTS

# INTRODUCTION

*"I have so much to do that I shall spend the
first three hours in prayer."*
                                    *-Martin Luther*

Time. It is your most precious commodity. It is more valuable than
huge sums of money or any amount of material possessions; yet most
people would rather spend time in an effort to save money, which
means that to them, their money is worth more than their time. A
truly prosperous person, however, understands the value of time, and
that every passing second is one that has never before existed, nor
ever will again. This person would rather spend money in an effort
to save time. The richest people are those who possess the most time.

When you begin to live with the belief that your time is precious and
valuable, you'll find yourself becoming increasingly aware of how
much time you have, how you're spending it, and the lengths you
would go to keep from wasting it. But beware of the fine line between
valuing time and being dominated by the unyielding pressure of the
ticking clock.

People all over the world woke up today with the belief that there just
isn't enough time in the day to do what needs to be done. So, from
the moment their feet hit the floor, they've been running as though
the alarm clock was a gunshot signaling the start of a day-long race.
Bang! And it's the sprint to get ready, the mad dash to school, leaping
over hurdles to the office, the dry cleaners, the doctor's appointment,

then back to the house with take-out again for dinner. But the clear problem with spending every waking moment on ourselves is that there are no moments left to give to God.

There was never a human being more aware of the ticking clock than Jesus. He had only a few short years to say what needed to be said and do what needed to be done. But somehow He did it. He managed to heal the sick, raise the dead, preach the gospel, and save humanity through His own death, burial, resurrection, and ascension, all in less time than it takes to graduate high school. And if you were to ask Jesus to tell you His secret to the mastery of time management, He would say, "It's simple. I only say what I hear My Father say, and I only do what I see My Father do."

You and I must make that our mode of operation, too. But how will you ever hear your Father say anything unless you take time to listen? I know, I know, you want to spend time seeking God, but it feels like there's a million other things that won't get done if you're sitting still reading your Bible. The truth is, time spent seeking God is never wasted time.

This book is a tool to help you seek Him. There are 52 devotions here, one for each week of the year. We encourage you to read them with an open heart; to use the journaling space provided at the end of each entry to write down what the Holy Spirit is saying to you through what you read; and to ask Him how He would have you be a doer of that word you've heard. Read in faith. Read with expectation to receive something good from God. Read with confidence, knowing that seekers always prosper.

"But without faith it is impossible to please Him, for he who comes to God must believe that He is, and that He is a rewarder of those who diligently seek Him." Hebrews 11:6

# 1

## THE FACE OF GOD

*"But we all, with unveiled face, beholding as in a mirror*
*the glory of the Lord, are being transformed into the same*
*image from glory to glory, just as by the Spirit of the Lord."*
*2 Corinthians 3:18 (NKJV)*

In Exodus 33, Moses was having an argument with God that almost got him killed. Things were going well for Moses, and God had said some wonderful things to him like, "You have also found grace in My sight" (v. 12), and "My Presence will go with you, and I will give you rest" (v. 14). Moses was living dangerously close to a New Testament experience; He had found grace, rest, and the constant presence of God—things that belong to you and me today but only through the finished work of Jesus. With things going strongly in his favor, he decided to go all-in and ask for, well, everything. In Exodus 33:18, Moses said, "Please, show me Your glory." God's response to Moses' brash request was, in essence, "Uh, no. You cannot see my face;" He said, "for no man shall see Me, and live" (Exodus 33:20). Essentially, God was saying to Moses, "I could show you, but then I'd have to kill you."

Second Corinthians 3:7-18 tells us that whatever did take place on the mountain that day was enough to make Moses shine. But according to verse 7, he was shining with a glory that was passing away. These verses are a comparison of two glories. One resulted from the "ministry of death, written and engraved on stones" (v. 7), and another resulted from the ministry of the Spirit—the ministry of righteousness (vs. 8-9).

Moses had to put a veil over his face to hide a glory that was passing away. In contrast, verse 18 tells us that because of Jesus, the veil has been removed, and "we all, with unveiled face, beholding as in a mirror the glory of the Lord, are being transformed into the same image from glory to glory, just as by the Spirit of the Lord" (v. 18); and only a few verses later we read,

*For it is the God who commanded light to shine out of darkness, who has shone in our hearts to give the light of the knowledge of the glory of God in the face of Jesus Christ.*

*2 Corinthians 4:6*

Moses asked to see the glory, and God said, "You cannot see My face." But we have moved *from* glory *to* glory. The veil has been removed; and now God is giving to you and me the light of the knowledge of the Glory found only in one place - in the face of Jesus Christ. We get to see what Moses asked to see but was denied. We get to see the face of the Glory Himself. When you look in the mirror, you are beholding (reflecting) the face of Jesus.

We no longer have to beg God to show us His glory. He has given us Jesus, and all we need to do is look to Him to see the full glory of the Father. In John 14:21 Jesus said, "He who has My commandments and keeps them, it is he who loves Me. And he who loves Me will be loved by My Father, and I will love him and manifest Myself to him." A manifestation of Jesus is a manifestation of the glory of God. Do you need healing? Look straight into the face of the Glory. Are you looking for peace? Look into the face of Jesus our Prince of Peace. Whatever it is you need, look no further than to Jesus. Spend time today beholding Him in His word and be changed from glory to glory. What you behold, you will become.

# *JOURNAL*

_____

_____

_____

_____

_____

_____

_____

_____

_____

_____

_____

_____

_____

_____

_____

_____

_____

_____

_____

_____

_____

_____

_____

_____

_____

_____

_____

_____

_____

# 2

## FEEDING ON HIS FAITHFULNESS

*"Trust in the Lord, and do good; Dwell in the land, and feed on His faithfulness." Psalm 37:3 (NKJV)*

Jeremy and I have made it a priority in our house to feed on His faithfulness by taking Communion together. At the slightest prompting, we gather whatever elements we can find, grab hands, and meet with Jesus around His Communion table. We stare into His face and literally feast on His body broken for us and His blood spilled for us. We remember what He went through so that we could be forgiven and made whole. We call to mind our history with Him and how He has been faithful time and time again.

When our son Justus was three years old, he started to run a fever so high that for the first time in his life he put himself to bed. We sensed the severity of the situation and knew it was time to run to the Communion table. As we met with Jesus, His sweet presence filled our house. We knew that He had been with us, and we were confident He was working in our little boy. The next morning Justus woke up perfectly fine, no sign of a fever! To our amazement, we found out a week later that he had been exposed to a highly contagious illness that broke out in our community. Every person who had the virus started out with a high fever like Justus did. This could have been serious for us since we had a brand-new baby at home, but just one meal with Jesus changed everything!

This meal becomes a covenant exchange where you get what you don't deserve. He takes your sin and gives you grace. He takes your sickness and gives you life. Jesus said, "Behold, I stand at the door and knock. If anyone hears My voice and opens the door, I will come in to him and dine with him, and he with Me" (Revelation 3:20). There is nothing like having dinner with Jesus.

I want to encourage you to take some time today to dine with Him and feast on His faithfulness. To feed is simply to eat or to take food. Jesus calls himself the bread of life and then clearly demonstrates to us how to take Communion. In 1 Corinthians 11:24-25, He gives thanks, breaks bread, and says, "Take, eat; this is my body which is broken for you; do this in remembrance of Me." Then he takes the cup saying, "This cup is the new covenant in My blood. This do, as often as you drink it, in remembrance of Me."

Did you notice how many times I mentioned the word take in the last paragraph? Even Jesus tells us to take and eat! That's because faith takes all that grace makes! When you take and eat the bread, see His healing love going to work in your body. When you take the cup and drink, see his mercy flowing through your veins. Take joy, take peace, take healing, take it all! Take your mind off yourself and what you've done wrong, and focus in on Jesus and everything He's done right. Remember Jesus, give thanks for Jesus, feed on Jesus, and you can be sure of one thing - you will always be well-fed.

# *JOURNAL*

---

# 3

## ANSWER THE MAN

*"Look at the birds of the air, for they neither sow nor reap nor gather into barns; yet your heavenly Father feeds them. Are you not of more value than they?"*
*Matthew 6:26 (NKJV)*

Jesus preached a powerful message in Matthew six that culminated in verse 33 with the immortal words, "Seek first the kingdom of God and His righteousness, and all these things shall be added to you." He was speaking to people about living life in a different manner than those without a relationship with God, who worry, strain, and strive for their food, their clothing, and every other need. He's letting us know there is supposed to be a difference between us and them. Throughout the passage He asked a number of questions, each one deserving of an answer from us. His questions weren't rhetorical, and how we answer them can dictate whether we live burdened with care, anxiety, and stress, or live supernaturally free from the weight of worry.

In verse 26, He told us to look at the birds of the air. If Jesus tells you to look at the birds, then you'd better look at the birds. He said they are not out there sowing and reaping or gathering into barns. In other words, they aren't working for a living or striving to put food in the nest. So how do they eat? Your heavenly Father feeds them. He then asks you the all-important question, "Are you not of more value than they?" If you can answer this question correctly, then you can live without giving another second to an anxious, worried thought. The question He's asking is, "Do you have any idea what you're worth?"

An object is given a value the moment a price is paid for it. In that instant, it's worth what the buyer is willing to give, even if it is to no one else but the one who bought it. Simply put, the price paid determines the value. Do you know that a price has been paid for you? Do you know the value that has been placed on your life? Do you know how precious you are to your heavenly Father? The Bible tells us in 1 Corinthians 6:20 that "you were bought at a price." And 1 Peter 1:18-19 says that we weren't redeemed with silver or gold but with the precious blood of Christ. Your value has been determined by the price that was paid for you, and the only One who gets to determine your value is the One who was willing to pay that price. No one else on earth has the right to determine your worth because they didn't pay for you.

What do you do with the most valuable things you possess? You take care of them. My friend, you are very, very expensive. In fact, you are the most valuable thing God owns; and like you, He takes care of what is most valuable. He is your caretaker because of how valuable you are to Him, and if you really knew how valuable you are to Him, then you'd never give another worried thought to meeting your own need.

Say it out loud right now: "I am worth the price that was paid for me. I am worthy because He made me worthy. My Father knows what I have need of before I even ask, and He meets that need because I am precious and valuable to Him." Jesus is asking you today, "Do you know how valuable you are?" I suggest you answer the Man.

# *JOURNAL*

# 4

A COLLISION WITH KINDNESS

*"...that in the ages to come He might show the exceeding riches of His grace in His kindness toward us in Christ Jesus." Ephesians 2:7 (NKJV)*

The word *loving-kindness* is two words tied together: loving and kindness. To me, loving-kindness means you can never separate His love from His kindness. The Lord declares through Psalm 89:33, "Nevertheless My loving-kindness I will not utterly take from him, nor allow My faithfulness to fail."

Do you remember Naomi in the Book of Ruth? After losing her husband and two sons, she is left in a foreign country with her two widowed daughters-in-law. She hears people talking about how the Lord is providing food for the people of Israel, and just hearing of His kindness begins to stir in her the desire to return home.

Jeremiah 31:3 says, "The Lord has appeared of old to me, saying: 'Yes, I have loved you with an everlasting love; therefore with loving-kindness I have drawn you.'" I am convinced that the Lord's kindness is the way He hooks us, changes us, and causes us to come back home to Him. Romans 2:4 says, "The goodness (kindness) of God leads you to repentance" (parenthesis mine). Fear of judgment may cause people to turn back to God, but it is only His kindness that keeps us.

One night as I was putting my little boy, Justus, to bed, I said, "I love you, buddy." I so badly wanted him to respond with, "I love you, too,

Mommy." When he didn't say it, I felt the need to solicit a response from him. I thought, *This will be an excellent time to teach and train him*, "When Mommy says *I love you*, you say, 'I love you, too, Mommy.'" But before I could get those words out of my mouth, the Lord checked my heart and I heard the still small voice inside say, "Never force him to say *I love you* back. It will mean more to you when he says it of his own free will and from his heart."

I realized that even if Justus never said *I love you* back to me, I would still spend my whole life proving my love to him. We know from Ephesians 2:7 that our Father will spend the ages to come showing us "the exceeding riches of His grace in His kindness toward us in Christ Jesus."

Kindness is also one of God's secrets to living a long life. Not long ago, I returned to the church I grew up in to minister at a conference. Before the service, I said hello to a 95-year-old lady on the second row. Throughout the years, I always noticed her quiet demeanor, sweet smile, and kind eyes. The pastor said to me, "Sarah, you remember Alice, right? You know as long as I've known her, I've never heard her say an unkind word about anyone."

God's kindness flowing to us and through us every day will produce life in our souls and in our bodies. It is only after we have a collision with His kindness that we are able to be genuinely kind to others. Think about what happens when two objects collide: an impact is made.

Never forget that His loving-kindness is always comforting, protecting, satisfying, and providing for you. Let His kindness draw you home today and be quick to recognize and respond. When you collide with the kindness, it will set in motion a chain reaction. You're now on a collision course to impact a world with the kindness of your Savior.

# *JOURNAL*

---

---

---

---

---

---

---

---

---

---

---

---

---

---

---

---

---

---

---

---

---

---

---

---

---

# 5

## ANOTHER WAY OUT

*"But we have this treasure in earthen vessels, that the excellence of the power may be of God and not of us. We are hard-pressed on every side, yet not crushed; we are perplexed, but not in despair; persecuted, but not forsaken; struck down, but not destroyed"*
*2 Corinthians 4:7-9 (NKJV)*

Have you ever felt like you are living life hard-pressed on every side? That's when you are up against some serious, unrelenting, unyielding pressure coming at you from every direction. Many people live their lives dealing on a daily basis with financial pressures, relational pressures, or pressures at work and home. You'll notice that when the pressure is on and at its worst, it will present you with, at the most, two bad choices - then demand that you choose now! Though it may feel like you've been backed into a corner and your choices are seemingly limited, just know you do not have to respond to the pressure. There is another way out.

Shortly after Pharaoh let Moses and the children of Israel leave Egypt, he changed his mind and started chasing them down. In Exodus 14, we see God's chosen people in a pretty tight spot and under some intense pressure. With the Red Sea in front of them and Pharaoh's army behind them, they began to cry out in fear and anger saying to Moses, "Did you bring us out here to die? It would've been better to be slaves in Egypt than to die in the wilderness!" They were pressed on all sides, and the pressure told them there were only two choices: be slaves or drown in the sea. But in Exodus 14:13-14 Moses said to the people, "Do not be afraid. Stand still, and see the salvation of the Lord, which He will accomplish for you today... The Lord will fight for you, and you shall hold your peace." The *Amplified Classic* translation says in verse fourteen, "The Lord will fight for you, and you shall hold your peace and remain at rest." That night the presence of God stood between them and Pharaoh's army while the Red Sea was being split in two, so they could walk across on dry land. You see, pressure had come and told them they had two choices: slavery or death. But faith in God gave them a supernatural way out - a way that no one would've considered to be an option or even a possibility; but it would require them to be still, hold their peace, and remain at rest. There is great power and a way of escape here in this simple instruction.

Be still. Being still is an act of faith, especially when you are under intense pressure and your mind and body are spinning trying to figure a way out. You don't have to let the pressure tell you where to go or what to do. You can be just like Jesus - don't do anything until you see your Father do it.

When Moses told them to "hold their peace" he was literally saying, "Be quiet!" When you give voice to the fear associated with the pressure, then you are allowing peace to escape you. Don't spend time talking about the problem and the pressure. Instead, be just like Jesus - don't say anything until you hear your Father say it.

The grace you need to lift you above the pressure can only go to work when you are at rest. So take your God-given place of rest—seated with Jesus in heavenly places—and say this out loud: "Grace is working. I am resting."

Even when the pressure is on, you can rest assured that God always has another way out. Just be still, hold your peace, and remain at rest.

# *J O U R N A L*

---

# 6

## GOD'S FAVORITE INSTRUMENT

*"For the eyes of the Lord run to and fro throughout the whole earth, to show Himself strong on behalf of those whose heart is loyal to Him..." 2 Chronicles 16:9 (NKJV)*

King David is one of the great figures in all the Bible. What a life he lived! He was a war hero to his generation, yet he was known as the sweet psalmist of Israel. He was full of courage yet admired for his gentleness. He started as a shepherd, and out of his legacy came a Savior.

What was it in David that made him great? What was it about him that so captured the heart of God? When choosing a king to rule over Israel, why did God pass over everyone else in David's family and stop at him and declare, "Arise, anoint him; for this is the one" (1 Samuel 16:12)?

We find the answer in 1 Samuel 16:7 when God refuses one of David's brothers and tells the prophet, "Do not look at his appearance or at his physical stature, because I have refused him. For the Lord does not see as man sees; for man looks at the outward appearance, but the Lord looks at the heart."

I am convinced that God chose David for one reason alone. It wasn't his physical appearance, his talents, or his gifts that drew God. It was his heart.

The heart is a big deal to God. In fact, the word *heart* is mentioned over 800 times in Scripture. Any number of heart conditions can exist inside a man. A heart can be cold and hard, or a heart can be warm and tender. Jesus even taught, "Blessed are the pure in heart, for they shall see God" (Matthew 5:8).

When it comes to ministering in music, I've found that whatever is going on in the chambers of the heart will affect the sound that comes out. Several years ago, I experienced this at the end of a service that we were ministering in. I was playing the piano while Jeremy was speaking, and on the inside, I heard the Lord say to me, "I want you to play what he is saying." Well how do you do that? It sounds crazy to the natural mind, right? But then I realized that there was no way I could do this from my head; I had to play from my heart. The instrument of the worshipper is not the guitar, piano, drums, or voice. The instrument of the worshipper is the heart.

The heart is the deepest part of us, the part that makes us who we are. It's where we believe, where we choose, where we feel, and where we love. In Psalm 42:7, David cries out, "Deep calls to deep in the roar of your waterfalls; all your waves and breakers have swept over me."

The deepest place in David calls for the deepest place in God, and his heart condition captures God's attention. In response, God Himself comes running after David. It's amazing to think that "the eyes of the Lord run to and fro throughout the whole earth, to show Himself strong on behalf of those whose heart is loyal to Him" (2 Chronicles 16:9).

Maybe you, like so many others, have been afraid to sing out because you don't like the way your voice sounds. Let me encourage you not to hold back. Turn the volume up on your heart because that's all God really wants to hear anyway.

# JOURNAL

_____
_____
_____
_____
_____
_____
_____
_____
_____
_____
_____
_____
_____
_____
_____
_____
_____
_____
_____
_____
_____
_____
_____
_____
_____
_____

# 7

## JUST JESUS

*"He who has My commandments and keeps them, it is he who loves Me. And he who loves Me will be loved by My Father, and I will love him and manifest Myself to him."*
*John 14:21 (NKJV)*

What if there was one answer to every question? One solution to every problem? And what if you knew that one answer? You'd be rich! Let's look together at something Jesus said:

*"He who has My commandments and keeps them, it is he who loves Me. And he who loves Me will be loved by My Father, and I will love him and manifest Myself to him."*
*John 14:21*

I dare you to come up with a question, a problem, a challenge of any kind that couldn't be radically turned around by a manifestation of Jesus. Maybe it's a sickness or disease of some kind? No. Healing is a manifestation of Jesus. What about a really "serious" financial hardship? Are you staring at a huge stack of overdue bills, school loans, or credit card debt? If so, let me tell you what you need. You need a manifestation of Jesus—the One who was rich but for your sake became poor, that you, through His poverty, might be made rich! Perhaps there are relationship-ending levels of strife in your life. There's an answer for that: a manifestation of Love Himself, Jesus.

In church, we've become so accustomed to hearing sermons that give us our "3 Steps to Victory," "6 Keys to Receiving," or the "12 Habits of Successful Saints." While there's nothing wrong with steps, keys, or principles, I need to remind you that none of it works apart from Jesus! The principle is powerless apart from the Person! Simply applying your best effort to any given problem is "3 steps" toward total failure in the eyes of God. In His eyes, you are either working for it, or resting in Him. But it can't be both.

The one thing you are in need of is a manifestation of Jesus. You need Him to show, reveal, and manifest Himself to you. What you need is for Jesus to let Himself be clearly seen by you, and for Him to make Himself real to you. The good news is, according to John 14:21, this is exactly what He wants to do!

So, what is the One answer to every question? Just Jesus. How about the One solution to every problem? Just Jesus. The knowledge of this One answer makes you and me very, very, very rich!

According to this verse, Jesus is in manifestation, first of all, in the life of anyone who has His commandments and keeps them. That means His words are more valuable to you than any other words, feelings, or emotions. But notice what else this manifestation of Jesus is connected to. He said "I will love him and manifest Myself to him." His manifested presence in your life is intimately and inseparably connected to a revelation of how much He loves you! So, get your affection off of the problem and start meditating and talking about how much Jesus loves you!

# JOURNAL

_____

_____

_____

_____

_____

_____

_____

_____

_____

_____

_____

_____

_____

_____

_____

_____

_____

_____

_____

_____

_____

_____

_____

_____

# 8

## ASK BIG!

*"... Yet you do not have because you do not ask."*
**James 4:2 (NKJV)**

The scriptures are full of faith heroes whose life stories are recorded for our benefit to strengthen our faith. Queen Esther gives us a great example of how to present our petitions to the Lord. She hears about the decree to destroy the Jews from her uncle Mordecai when he pleads with her to go into the king and petition him to save her people. At first she is unsure, unsettled, and reluctant to go because she does not know the king's heart on the matter. To enter into the king's inner court without being called for could very likely mean death for her. But Mordecai encourages her to press past her fear of death and ask big. He says, "For if you remain completely silent at this time, relief and deliverance will arise for the Jews from another place, but you and your father's house will perish. Yet who knows whether you have come to the kingdom for such a time as this?" (Esther 4:14).

The first step in presenting your petition is to speak up and ask. So many people never see the desires of their hearts because they don't stop to ask. James 4:2 says, "You do not have because you do not ask."

Esther is slow and strategic with her petition. She doesn't freak out when she hears the bad report, and she doesn't run to the king frantically begging for his help. She calls for a fast and seeks the Lord. Then she "put on her royal robes and stood in the inner court of the king's palace," and when he sees her "standing in the court, that she found favor in his sight" saying to her, "'What do you wish, Queen Esther? What is your request? It shall be given to you—up to half the kingdom!'" (Esther 5:1-3).

Now, because of Jesus, we have it even better than Esther! We are to come boldly before His throne of grace wearing our royal robes of righteousness, being fully aware that He loves us, knowing His favor goes before us and that His greatest desire is to give us the riches of His kingdom!

At the sound of bad news, we should never fly off the handle, fearfully spouting off scriptures and confessions without any power. Esther takes her time with the king, arranges several encounters with him, and creates opportunities to find and discover his will in the situation. And when she is convinced of his love for her and his willingness to bless her, then she presents her petition. "If it pleases the king, and if I have found favor in his sight and the thing seems right to the king...let it be written to revoke the letters...which [Haman] wrote to annihilate the Jews" (Esther 8:5).

Esther doesn't march in demanding that he grant her desires, but with a humble heart and with great honor, she solicits his will on the subject. Notice she says, "If it pleases the king... and the thing seems right to the king."

We shouldn't just want our way; we should want His will. First John 5:14-15 says, "Now this is the confidence that we have in Him, that if we ask anything according to His will, He hears us. And if we know that He hears us, whatever we ask, we know that we have the petitions that we have asked of Him."

In the end, Esther finds favor with the King. He grants her request and her people are saved!

Don't be afraid to ask big! Approach your Father's throne with great confidence knowing that you are loved and favored by the King, and it is His delight to give you His kingdom.

## *J O U R N A L*

_____

_____

_____

_____

_____

_____

_____

_____

_____

_____

_____

_____

_____

_____

_____

_____

_____

_____

_____

# 9

## IT'S TIME TO EAT

*"David said, 'Trust in the Lord, and do good; dwell in the land, and feed on His faithfulness'" Psalms 37:3 (NKJV)*

Who doesn't enjoy a good meal? As a matter of fact, if you're hungry right now, then let me give you something to chew on.

In Psalms 37:3, David said, *"Trust in the Lord, and do good; dwell in the land, and feed on His faithfulness."* There's nothing more satisfying than the faithfulness of God, and we must never stop feeding on it! Trust me, when you are feeding on how faithful He has been to you, you are never in danger of overeating.

I want you to notice the context that this verse comes to us in and the verses that lead up to it. In Psalm 37:1-2 (NLT), he says:

*Don't worry about the wicked or envy those who do wrong. For like grass, they soon fade away. Like spring flowers, they soon wither.*

"Trust in the Lord," he said, "and do good." Doing good is simply doing what He's called you to do. His instruction here is also to "dwell in the land." That means we are supposed to go where He has called us to go. When we go where He has called us to go and do what He has called us to do, we can be sure that in that place His faithfulness will put food on the table and clothes on our backs. First Thessalonians 5:24 says, *"He who calls you is faithful, who also will do it."*

Your Father God has prepared a table before you, even in the presence of your enemies. So what are you waiting for? Pull up a chair and start feeding on every good and perfect gift that He has already given you. The best place to start is in thanking Him for Jesus. Jesus Christ is faithfully the same yesterday, today, and forever. He is the faithfulness of God to you. Then take a look at everything He is doing for you right now. Maybe you aren't yet where you want to be in life, but He has been faithful to bring you up out of the mess you were in and set your feet on solid ground. Dig in to the sweet things that are yet to come. If He did it for you, then you know He will do it again because God is faithful. That means He does not change, He will not quit, and He cannot fail. He's faithful, now let's eat!

# *JOURNAL*

---

---

---

---

---

---

---

---

---

---

---

---

---

---

---

---

---

---

---

---

---

---

---

---

---

---

---

# 10

## ACCORDING TO YOUR FAITH

*"Let us therefore come boldly to the throne of grace, that*
*we may obtain mercy and find grace to help in time of*
*need." Hebrews 4:16 (NKJV)*

If you are standing and believing for healing for yourself or for your child, remember the story of the Canaanite woman in Matthew 15:21-28, who falls at Jesus' feet in need of healing for her daughter. It seems puzzling to hear our kind and merciful Jesus refuse her request for mercy when he says to her, "I was not sent except to the lost sheep of the house of Israel." He then appears to put her down by calling her an animal, "It is not good to take the children's bread and throw it to the dogs." This doesn't sound like our loving grace-filled Jesus, does it? He says it, so there must be something for us to see.

This woman is a Gentile, an outsider from the family of God. In fact she comes from a long line of people who worshipped other gods. She is completely undeserving and doesn't have a right to ask for healing because she isn't from the House of Israel. But with a humble heart she agrees with Jesus, "Yes Lord, yet even the little dogs eat the crumbs which fall from their master's table." She chooses to believe that there is enough healing in Jesus that even just a crumb will fix her unworthy family.

Jesus is amazed by her great faith, and her little girl is healed!

Despite appearances Jesus isn't being mean to her at all. He is showing us even more about His amazing grace; that we don't receive according to what we deserve, we receive according to our faith in Jesus!

This is good news! Your sinful past cannot keep you from receiving healing! The only thing that can hold you out is refusing to believe. Jesus has made a way for us to "come boldly before his throne of Grace" and take all the healing mercies that we need.

I've seen some of the greatest miracles happen in my life the moment I come to the end of myself and choose to rely fully on Him. Healing comes when you stop focusing on yourself and what you can do to fix it, and start staring at Jesus and everything He has done to finish it.

One evening, I began to have severe pain in my stomach. I have learned from experience that if I want to receive healing I cannot stare at my symptoms and my Savior at the same time. I began to worship, and let the eyes of my heart focus in on Jesus. Each wave of pain was fighting for my attention, but I knew I had to keep my mind on My healer. After about 10 minutes of singing and worshipping Him and refusing to pay attention to the symptoms, the pain completely left. The still small voice of the Lord spoke to my heart, "If I can capture your stare, I can change your circumstance."

When you are in the middle of a miracle, the devil will try to come and remind you of your failures and mistakes, and make you feel completely unworthy of healing. But remember you do not receive anything from God because you deserve it. You receive according to your faith. Set your eyes on Jesus today and let His healing mercies flow!

# *JOURNAL*

_____

_____

_____

_____

_____

_____

_____

_____

_____

_____

_____

_____

_____

_____

_____

_____

_____

_____

_____

_____

_____

_____

_____

_____

_____

# 11

## SAY WHAT?

*"I tell you the truth, you can say to this mountain, 'May you be lifted up and thrown into the sea,' and it will happen. But you must really believe it will happen and have no doubt in your heart.'" Mark 11:23 (NLT)*

The days in which you and I live are unlike any this world has ever seen. For believers, it is of the utmost importance that we learn to live with purpose and precision.

There is no more time for a "win some, lose some" way of thinking. We are winners, champions, and more than conquerors through Him who loves us. But champions don't have the luxury of laying around doing nothing. They train. They study. They practice. They rehearse. They build in themselves a new nature, a new way of thinking, and a new set of instincts that will respond correctly in any situation without hesitation or doubt. To live with the precision of a champion will require mind renewal and an overhaul in the way we talk.

If we are going to have good communication with God, we must learn to speak His language—Faith. Faith is the only language God speaks. He does not speak worry, fear, or beggar, or any other language contrary to what you read in His word. You and I can learn to speak other languages, but God will speak faith and faith alone from now until eternity. If you want to understand Him, you must learn to speak the same language.

Our words of faith carry great power. If they didn't, you and I could not be saved. Anyone who was ever born again got that way by believing in their heart and confessing with their mouth that Jesus is Lord. "For with the heart one believes unto righteousness, and with the mouth confession is made unto salvation" (Romans 10:10).

The word confession literally means "to say the same thing as." This is why the potential for great power exists in the words of your mouth. You were saved by the miraculous love and power of God when you simply said the same thing (confessed) about Jesus that God said about Him.

This same principle must be followed in the way we live after we make that powerful confession. Instead of just throwing out a shotgun prayer or yelling scriptures real loud, take the time to find out from God what He is saying about the situation. Then be a believer of that Word, and respond to it by coming into agreement with it and saying what He's said.

No matter what you are facing, every situation requires one thing above all others: a listening ear. Wouldn't you like to know what God thinks about what you are going through? Wouldn't you like to get His thoughts on the matter? Then you'll have to get quiet, and listen. There is no power in what you say until you are saying the same thing that God says. In Mark 11:23 Jesus said, "Whoever says to this mountain…" then told us exactly what to say. What is your response? You believe because He said it, and because of that belief you are going to say exactly what He said. Nothing more. Nothing less. That is a confession. And that is precision living.

So find out what God has already said about you, and say that. Find out what His Word has to say about your situation. When you do, respond to it in faith—believing and confessing. If you aren't sure yet what to say, then simply go before the Lord and say, "Father, what do

You say about this? And what do You want me to say about it?" Once you hear, then say what you heard Him say and nothing else. Come into agreement with God as you learn to speak His language.

## *JOURNAL*

_____

_____

_____

_____

_____

_____

_____

_____

_____

_____

_____

_____

_____

_____

_____

_____

_____

_____

_____

_____

# 12

## THANKSGIVING THERAPY

*"Bless the Lord, O my soul, And forget not all His benefits: Who forgives all your iniquities, Who heals all your diseases..." Psalm 103:2-3 (NKJV)*

After having my second baby, I was exhausted and worn down from all the sleepless nights and a reaction to a medicine I had taken. I needed help and healing and I knew it was time to press in like never before. One night as I lay in bed, I asked the Lord to give me a practical way to receive, and He was faithful to answer.

"Thanksgiving therapy," He said.

I knew in my heart what this meant. I needed to come to Him several times a day and do nothing but meditate on His Word, remember His loving-kindness, and thank Him for the good things He had done for me.

Therapy is simply a treatment for a disease or a remedy for a disorder. The Greek word *therapia* literally means healing.

If you want to be well, you have to make an appointment with a physician. If the desire to be healed is strong enough, you will find time and make it an absolute priority. You must find a quiet place where you can both talk and listen. And lastly, you have to be consistent with the therapy sessions in order for them to be effective. It is the one who is constant in believing, unwavering with the word, and fully persuaded of His promise that sees results in the end.

I began to set appointments with the Great Physician, where I would lie down and quiet my soul. I would close my eyes and remember specific moments in my past when God overwhelmed me with His love, and began to thank Him for each one. I would recall stories from my childhood. As I called to mind our history, I realized that each memory was a victory, and my thankful heart became alive with praise. His love flooded my soul, and I knew that fear was being forced out and healing was working in me.

Memories are extremely powerful. Scientists and doctors have discovered a concept they call "cellular memory," where the body stores pictures of life events or memories within the cells. Many believe that hurtful memories, if not healed, can eventually be destructive to a person's health. But we have the ability to use our memory for good, and when we do, healing occurs. Psalm 103:2-3 says, "Bless the Lord, O my soul, and forget not (in other words *remember*) all His benefits: Who forgives all your iniquities, Who heals all your diseases."

During my times in thanksgiving therapy, I thought about all the good times with God. I set my mind on Jesus, His finished work on the cross, and His healing words to me. Just like in natural therapy appointments, I noticed myself crying during the first sessions. The truth is, crying isn't always a sign of weakness. Oftentimes it's a sign of healing where the calloused places of the heart are becoming soft and tender once again.

Think about the ten lepers who were all miraculously healed. Only one of them took the time to go back and say *thank you* to Jesus; and as a result, he was made completely whole. Thanksgiving will make you whole just like it did for him. Make an appointment with your great physician today. He is waiting for your call.

# JOURNAL

_____

_____

_____

_____

_____

_____

_____

_____

_____

_____

_____

_____

_____

_____

_____

_____

_____

_____

_____

_____

_____

_____

_____

_____

# 13

## REVIVE

*"I am afflicted very much; Revive me, O Lord, according to Your word." Psalm 119:107 (NKJV)*

Have you ever felt like you don't have the strength, the determination, or the drive that you once had in your life? My friend, we have all been there. Even the faith-hero King David of the Bible was there on more than one occasion, and yet the story of his life is one of triumph over trial, and victory over adversity. Take a look at these verses he wrote from Psalm 119, and try to pick up on the recurring theme.

*(v. 25) My soul clings to the dust;*
*Revive me according to Your word.*

*(v. 37) Turn away my eyes from looking at worthless things,*
*And revive me in Your words.*

*(v. 107) I am afflicted very much;*
*Revive me, O Lord, according to Your word.*

*(v. 154) Plead my cause and redeem me;*
*Revive me according to Your word.*

It seems to me that David knew a thing or two about being worn out, worn down, and beat up by life. But it's also apparent that he wasn't willing to stay that way. When his soul was trying its best to cling to the dust, or when the affliction against him was at its worst, he cried out to God "Revive me with Your word!"

The word "revive" found here in the *New King James Version* is also translated quicken, or to make alive. It is a giant word that carries with it not only the idea of having life, but also that of being brought back to life. It brings to my mind the image of a defibrillator - the device we've all seen used on countless medical television dramas when a person dies. The doctor or nurse reaches for the two paddles connected by electrical cords to a small box, then yells, "Clear!" as they slam the paddles down on the patient's chest, sending enough voltage through their body to jump start a small car, all in an effort to get the heart beating again. The long, steady tone of death coming from the EKG machine is suddenly interrupted by a rhythmic, "Beep. Beep. Beep." And the one who was once dead has been revived.

You must live with the same revelation David lived with, knowing there is enough power in the Word of God to revive you and to get your heart beating again. I challenge you to lay in bed at night reading these words from Psalm 119, and imagine them having the same effect on your heart that 1,000 volts of electricity would have coursing through a once-dead body. There is no sense in you lying there on your bed each night, dying on the inside, while somewhere in your house there is a bible sitting still and closed, with enough power in it to jumpstart your heart and bring you back to life. Instead of looking at a bunch of worthless things on TV or the internet before you close your eyes tonight, "clear" everything else from your heart and mind, and put your attention on God's electrifying words of life.

# JOURNAL

---
---
---
---
---
---
---
---
---
---
---
---
---
---
---
---
---
---
---
---
---
---
---
---
---

# 14

## BEHOLD AND BECOME

*"So then faith comes by hearing, and hearing by the word of God." Romans 10:17 (NKJV)*

To behold Jesus is not to give Him a fleeting glance. Instead, it is to set aside time where He has your undivided attention, where you look at Him with a constant, immovable, and firm gaze. Remember the old saying—you become what you behold.

Several years ago while we were on a ministry trip in India, I heard a true story about a little girl who was born with four arms and four legs. She was named after a four-armed Hindu goddess, Lakshmi, who many in India worship as the goddess of wealth. People in her village started to worship this little girl along with other children who were born with deformities, believing they were reincarnated gods.

After hearing this story, I was riding down a crowded street in India, and I couldn't help but notice all of the businesses and buildings that were named after the original goddess Lakshmi and the billboards that boasted her picture. I remembered the deformed little girl who looked just like her and the doctors who were trying to reconstruct her body. The eyes of my heart came wide open, and I knew that this situation was much more spiritual than many had realized. These people had spent so much time beholding other gods that they opened themselves up to the spirits behind them, even to the point that their children were beginning to resemble the image of the gods they worshipped. The very flesh of this little girl had been transformed into the same image that her mother was constantly staring at. Her baby became what she beheld, and the same concept applies to us—whatever we stare at we give power to.

Second Corinthians 3:18 says, "But we all, with unveiled face, beholding as in a mirror the glory of the Lord, are being transformed into the same image from glory to glory, just as by the Spirit of the Lord."

What if Lakshmi's mother had spent time throughout her pregnancy staring at Jesus instead of beholding another god? I have no doubt that her situation would look drastically different. As we behold our Healer, we begin to look just like Him—a picture of health. After all, healing happens when we're with the Healer.

I woke up one morning tired from travel, in need of a real encounter with the Lord. I had spent time reading and confessing the Word but still felt emotional and worn down. I decided to turn on a teaching about seeing Jesus in every book of the Bible, and after only fifteen minutes of beholding Him in Scripture, I was supercharged! I could sense genuine faith rising up in my heart, and as I finished in prayer, I knew that there was power backing up my words. I was stirred up and completely confident that my prayer was working.

Romans 10:17 says, "So faith comes from hearing, that is, hearing the Good News about Christ."

Do you remember when Jesus met up with the two disciples on the road to Emmaus after He rose from the dead? "Their eyes were restrained, so that they did not know Him" (Luke 24:16), and they walked with Him for a while without recognizing Him. But then Jesus began to take them on an adventure, a Bible study "beginning at Moses and all the Prophets...[and] expounded to them in all the Scriptures the things concerning Himself" (Luke 24:27). As He spoke, the eyes of their hearts began to open and they saw Jesus for who He really was.

This week, take some extra time to set your eyes on Jesus. Behold Him and watch as your faith begins to soar!

## *J O U R N A L*

_____

_____

_____

_____

_____

_____

_____

_____

_____

_____

_____

_____

_____

_____

_____

_____

_____

_____

# 15

## HOW DO YOU PLEAD?

*"For God did not send His Son into the world to condemn the world, but that the world through Him might be saved." John 3:17 (NKJV)*

John 3:16. You know it. I know it. "For God so loved the world that He gave His only begotten Son, that whoever believes in Him should not perish but have everlasting life." But do you know John 3:17? "For God did not send His Son into the world to condemn the world, but that the world through Him might be saved."

It's one thing to tell someone you love them, but proving that love is something else entirely. Some people are all talk but offer no proof to back up their words. But not God. When He talks, His words do something, and when He says *I love you*, there is going to be proof that follows and backs up those words. John 3:17 is that proof.

Love sent Jesus to us, not to condemn us, but to save us from condemnation. "But I feel so guilty and condemned because I keep messing up with the same sin over and over, and I just know that God is mad at me." If that is what you've been saying, then it is obvious you are more aware of what you've done than you are of what Jesus has done.

You may have even been told you needed to feel guilty so that you would come back to God, but that is a lie! It's not guilt and shame that brings us to repentance. It is the kindness and goodness of God that leads men to change (Rom. 2:4). Condemnation that comes with the consciousness of your sin can't bring you to God; and, as a matter of fact, it will try to drive you away from Him.

One day, after Peter and the boys had been fishing all night and had caught nothing, Jesus told them to launch out again and let down their nets. When they did, they caught a boat-sinking load of fish, and to Peter, that was a boat full of money. That one catch could pay the mortgage, buy the groceries, fix the boat, and maybe even buy a new one.

You'd think that Peter would have been happy. He'd just met the Man that could keep his family fed forever. But what did he say to Jesus? "Depart from me, for I am a sinful man, O Lord!" (Luke 5:8). Sin consciousness can't separate God from you, but it tries to separate you from Him.

Satan is the accuser of the brethren, ever living to accuse you and to hold your sins against you. He is the prosecuting attorney that claims he has evidence against you—bad things you've said and done. But 1 John 2:1 says that if we sin, we have an Advocate with the Father, Jesus Christ the Righteous. We've got the greatest lawyer ever. And like any good lawyer would do, ours has given us the words to speak in response to the allegations against us; but you must stick to the script. Jesus said, "By your words you will be justified, and by your words you will be condemned" (Matt. 12:37). You can't start crying about how guilty and sinful you are. Your lawyer can't help you if you plead guilty. So what do you say when the Judge turns to you and asks, "How do you plead?" You very confidently and humbly say, "I plead the blood." If you confess anything, let it be the confession of your righteousness in Christ Jesus.

The only One with any right to condemn you, chose instead to justify and free you. Does God really love you? Yes. And there's your proof.

# JOURNAL

_____

_____

_____

_____

_____

_____

_____

_____

_____

_____

_____

_____

_____

_____

_____

_____

_____

_____

_____

_____

_____

_____

_____

# 16

## SINGING AND RECEIVING

*"...if you confess with your mouth the Lord Jesus and believe in your heart that God has raised Him from the dead, you will be saved. For with the heart one believes unto righteousness, and with the mouth confession is made unto salvation." Romans 10:9-10 (NKJV)*

Did you know you can sing sickness away? Singing is God's sedative for the soul and an expression of faith from the spirit. God loves music, but it's not just because it is fun to listen to or a good opening act before the Word is preached in a service. He loves it because He knows music from heaven brings healing. God designed music to help us receive everything He came to give.

I heard a true story that a father told about his little girl who was diagnosed with a severe digestive disease—severe to the point that the doctors were giving her little hope and no time to live. Most days she could hardly eat without having to rush to the bathroom in pain, and certainly she could eat nothing fun like cookies or cake. She seemed to get worse and worse day after day. Her parents took her to a meeting at a church, and at the end of the service, the minister called people up to receive prayer for healing. She went up and by faith took her healing that night. When she returned to her seat, she looked up and said, "Daddy, if I'm healed, then that means I can eat a cookie tonight, right?"

Her father admitted fighting feelings of fear as he thought about what she would potentially go through if she ate even one cookie. But for some reason, he knew that he could not tell her no because it would discourage her and tear down her simple faith in God as her healer. She was so excited about being healed that she believed she could eat a cookie without it affecting her. That night she still had pain and symptoms after she ate her cookie, but that was soon to change. For a long while, every night before bed, her parents would hear her in her room all by herself singing at the top of her lungs, "I'm healed, I'm healed, and I can eat cookies now! I'm healed, I'm healed, and I can eat cookies now!"

Time went on, and everyone noticed that she was gradually getting better and better. And then the little girl who was never supposed to grow up and live out her life did. On her wedding day, before she was about to walk down the aisle, she had a conversation with her father about her miracle healing as a little girl. She said, "Daddy, I never told you why I sang that song. Every night before bed, I would see angels in my room, and they would lead me in that song that went, 'I'm healed. I'm healed, and I can eat cookies now.'"

There is power when a song is sung in faith because we sing from the same place we believe from. The heart is where we love from, believe from, and sing from. Faith is of the heart! Romans 10:9-10, the great salvation chapter, says, "If you confess with your mouth the Lord Jesus and believe in your heart that God has raised Him from the dead, you will be saved. For with the heart one believes unto righteousness, and with the mouth confession is made unto salvation."

Your song may just be one of your greatest expressions of faith when it comes from the heart and when you sing it out loud. So go ahead, open your mouth and sing His Word! As you do, you will find that His presence is medicine to all your flesh.

# JOURNAL

_____
_____
_____
_____
_____
_____
_____
_____
_____
_____
_____
_____
_____
_____
_____
_____
_____
_____
_____
_____
_____
_____
_____
_____

# 17

## GRACE SAID, FAITH SAYS

*"If any of you lacks wisdom, let him ask of God, who gives*
*liberally and without reproach, and it will be given to him."*
*James 1:5 (NKJV)*

Sarah and I have had many great Bible teachers in our lives, but several years ago we were introduced to one of the best ever: our son, Justus. He has taught us so much about the Love of God and the heart of our Father.

For nearly a year after Justus arrived, he spoke to us mostly in squeals and grunts. That is until a few months later when, seemingly out of nowhere, he looked up and clearly said, "Dada." It's hard to even know how to put into words what that does to the heart of a parent.

The Lord began to reveal to us why it made us so happy to hear Justus say these little words. He said, "It pleases you because your son is learning to speak your language." Then He took us to Hebrews 11:6, where we find that without faith it is impossible to please God. Faith is the language God speaks. It's the only language He speaks, and it's the only language He understands.

Your entire relationship with God should be lived as an ongoing conversation between Grace and Faith. Grace is Him speaking to you, and faith is your response to Him. Faith is the language of the believer, which is who and what we are. We are believers, and we are not beggars!

It is vitally important that you begin to think and talk this way, because until you learn to speak faith, God can't understand what you are saying. But, the moment you call on Him in faith, you bring great joy to the heart of your Father because you, His child, are learning to speak His language.

Let's look at James 1:5-7 and you'll see exactly what we're saying.

*5 If any of you lacks wisdom, let him ask of God, who gives to all liberally and without reproach, and it will be given to him. 6 But let him ask in faith, with no doubting, for he who doubts is like a wave of the sea driven and tossed by the wind. 7 For let not that man suppose that he will receive anything from the Lord;*

Verse 5 is a demonstration of the character and will of God. He is generous and gracious, and loves nothing more than to give to His children. The promise here is that when you ask, it will be given to you.

Then comes verse 6, and even though we have a generous God who loves to lavishly supply, we see someone who has failed to receive from Him. Did His will to give suddenly change? Did He come up short and unable to supply? No way! He is always willing and He'll always have more than enough.

What we have here is a breakdown in communication. Whoever did the asking did not ask in faith. They weren't speaking God's language. Maybe they were begging God based on the need, or pleading with Him to act on their behalf. But He doesn't speak worry, fear or doubt, and He certainly doesn't speak beggar! If this person is ever going to receive from God what they are asking for, they must learn to ask in faith by responding to His grace.

*GRACE SAID, FAITH SAYS*

Whatever came to you through Jesus is grace! So, if it has already been provided, how do we ask? "Father, I want to thank You for the wisdom that You have made available to me through Jesus. I ask You for it, and I believe that I receive it from You." Now you are living in the conversation between grace and faith.

## JOURNAL

_____

_____

_____

_____

_____

_____

_____

_____

_____

_____

_____

_____

_____

_____

_____

_____

_____

_____

# 18

## GET YOUR OWN GOD

*"...I call to remembrance the genuine faith that is in you,*
*which dwelt first in your grandmother Lois and your*
*mother Eunice, and I am persuaded is in you also."*
*2 Timothy 1:5 (NKJV)*

It was 1986, and I was only three-years old. I don't remember a lot about that year other than my mom's giant rockstar hair, her sweet smile, and my very first moment with Jesus. I loved to sit in my room inside my little, plastic playhouse and watch *The Gospel Bill Show.* If you're not familiar with this television program, let me introduce you to my childhood. When my brothers came along, we didn't want to watch anything else. God used a man dressed up as a cowboy to preach the Gospel to millions of children all over the world, and I was one of them. I don't remember everything he said, but I'll never forget the moment the presence of the Lord filled up my room. The Holy Spirit reached down into my heart and lit a fire, and then I reached out by faith and took Him as my own.

Throughout the Psalms, David claims God as His own. He cries out, "O God, you are my God; early will I seek You; my soul thirsts for You; my flesh longs for you..." (Psalm 63:1-2).

When my mother was pregnant with me, she started bleeding. The doctors told her she was going to miscarry, but she stood on the Word, trusted God, and He came through for us, so I'm alive today. When I was four, I had scarlet fever and lost some of my eyesight and had to wear glasses. My mom, dad, grandma, and grandpa all came together and agreed in faith that I would be healed, and I was. I have perfect 20/20 vision today. When I was little, I was healed by the grace of God and my parents' and grandparents' faith. But there would come a time when I would need to develop a faith of my own.

Faith becomes real when it becomes yours. Paul saw this kind of real faith in Timothy and encouraged him when he said, "I call to remembrance the genuine faith that is in you, which dwelt first in your grandmother Lois and your mother Eunice, and I am persuaded is in you also" (2 Timothy 1:5).

Fast forward thirty years to when I was pregnant with my second baby. I began to bleed just like my mom did with me. As I lay in bed that night, fear tried to surround me. It was time for me to seek the Lord and receive my miracle. Throughout the night we stood on the Word and pressed in to prayer and praise like never before. By morning I had stopped bleeding, and when we arrived at the doctor's office, the ultrasound showed a perfectly healthy baby in my womb. I am so thankful that I had a God of my own who was there for me in a time of trouble.

There comes a time in your life when you have to develop your own faith in God if you want to receive all that He has planned for you. We all need our own living communion with Jesus, and from that fellowship, faith will freely flow. At some point, Momma's and Daddy's faith won't cut it. Grandma's and Grandpa's faith won't be enough. Not even your pastor or your friends will be able to carry you any further. You'll need faith of your own. Faith in God will give you a story that will give Him glory. So go ahead, get your own God! He's only a breath away, so reach out and take Him as your own.

# JOURNAL

_____
_____
_____
_____
_____
_____
_____
_____
_____
_____
_____
_____
_____
_____
_____
_____
_____
_____
_____
_____
_____
_____
_____
_____
_____
_____
_____

# 19

## THE SECRET TO
## YOUR SUCCESS

*"I know how to be abased, and I know how to abound.*
*Everywhere and in all things I have learned both to be full*
*and to be hungry, both to abound and to suffer need. I can*
*do all things through Christ who strengthens me."*
*Philippians 4:12-13 (NKJV)*

"Know how" in any given area of life can be priceless information. Paul said to his partners in the Philippian church, "I *know how* to be abased and I *know how* to abound." There are those that would read that verse and say, "I know plenty about being abased! I've got that part down, flat!" However, just because someone is abased, doesn't necessarily mean they know anything about "how" to do it the right way. If they never find out how to do it, then they are destined to live small and suffer need for the rest of their lives. Just because someone has a bunch of money and stuff, that doesn't mean they know a thing in the world about "how to abound." If they never learn how to truly abound, then they are destined to live without ever making a difference in the world around them.

While most people are only interested in knowing how to abound, I submit to you that unless you know how to be abased and be in faith at the same time, you will never know how to abound. But if you'll learn the how-to's and what-to-do's while being abased, then soon you'll be on the road to abounding and overflowing, which is where God has called you to be.

Philippians 4:12-13 in the *New Living Translation* says, "I know how to live on almost nothing or with everything. I have learned the secret of living in every situation, whether it is with a full stomach or empty, with plenty or little. For I can do everything through Christ, who gives me strength." The secret to life is living with the revelation you can do everything through Christ who gives you strength. Money or material things don't make you strong. No matter where you are on the road from abased to abounding, you must live your life being strengthened from the inside-out, not the outside-in.

Paul lived with this "know how" and that's why he could say to his partners, "I do not speak in regard to need" (verse 11). This is another tool you need to put in your belt if you are going to know how to be abased on your way to abounding. Make the decision now that you are going to stop speaking in regard to the need, and start speaking in regard to the One who supplies for the need. There is a big problem with talking about the need all the time when you're doing it in an effort to get another person to meet your need. That's called manipulation; and even if it works, you are immediately limited to what that person is able to do for you. But if you'll put the pressure on the Word to meet your need, then you'll tap into an unlimited source of the goodness of God that will cause you to abound beyond your need. As you begin to make your way out of the state of being abased and into the state of abounding, be assured that there will be those who see what's happening in your life and will want to know the secret to your success. Tell them your secret is that you can do all things through Christ Jesus, who is making you strong!

# *JOURNAL*

_____

_____

_____

_____

_____

_____

_____

_____

_____

_____

_____

_____

_____

_____

_____

_____

_____

_____

_____

_____

_____

_____

_____

_____

_____

# 20

## BETTER TOGETHER

*"God sets the solitary in families..." Psalm 68:6 (NKJV)*

God is all about family. The creation of Earth and man were about His overwhelming desire for fellowship, relationship, and closeness with us. However, when sin and death came on the scene, they created distance between us and Him. But right away the plan of redemption went into effect, and when Jesus died, so did the distance between God and man. It cost God everything He had, but to Him we were worth it. He had His family back.

Ephesians 2:14 (MSG) says, "The Messiah has made things up between us so that we're now together on this . . . . He tore down the wall we used to keep each other at a distance."

Don't you love it? Through Jesus, we're together with God again because we were never meant to be apart and alone. Psalm 68:6 says, "God sets the solitary in families." Giving someone a family is a sweet thought, but God wasn't just being nice when He did that. God set us in a family intending for us to build rich relationships with Him and with each other because of the power that comes from being together.

Over the past ten years, Jeremy and I have found that the power of God is at its strongest in our marriage, our family, and our ministry when we will simply get together on whatever it is we're believing

God to do for us. Jesus called it "the power of agreement," but we must all understand that there is just as much power working against us in our disagreement. No wonder the devil comes to stir up strife and create distance among people in families. His plan is to divide and conquer. He's after the family.

We should be living now more than ever before with an awareness of the enemy's attempts to rob our families of our God-intended closeness. I, for one, refuse to let him take from us the life that Jesus wants us to have and enjoy together.

On New Year's Eve 2015, my mom was diagnosed with terminal cancer and given ten months to live. As a family, we sought the Lord together. We prayed together. We came together in agreement over the healing of her body. All of us together said the same thing, "We will win!"

We took Jesus at His word and believed Him when He said, "If two of you agree on earth concerning anything that they ask, it will be done for them by My Father in heaven. For where two or three are gathered together in My name, I am there in the midst of them" (Matthew 18:19-20). Ten months later, all the scans and tests showed that there was no disease in her body. God was faithful, and together we won!

Never let the enemy convince you that you are alone. If you have received Jesus, you have been born again into the great big family of God! Find out who you are called to do life with and take advantage of the power of agreement. The truth is, we are all better together!

# JOURNAL

_____

_____

_____

_____

_____

_____

_____

_____

_____

_____

_____

_____

_____

_____

_____

_____

_____

_____

_____

_____

_____

_____

_____

# 21

## PATHFINDER

*"Your word is a lamp to my feet And a light to my path."*
*Psalm 119:105 (NKJV)*

You have been on God's mind for a long time. As a matter of fact, He's been thinking about you since before the foundation of the earth. The scriptures tell us that God never sleeps or slumbers. I believe that's because you and I are always on His mind, and He can't quit thinking about us. He couldn't go to sleep if He wanted to, because He'd just lay awake thinking about all the plans He has for your life. God spoke through His prophet in Jeremiah 29:11 and revealed just what He thinks when He thinks about you. *"For I know the thoughts that I think toward you, says the Lord, thoughts of peace and not of evil, to give you a future and a hope."* The *Amplified* translation says that He knows the thoughts and the plans that He has for you. So when He's thinking about you, He's not thinking about your past—He's planning for your future!

The number one way to find out what God's plan is for your future is to develop a love for His Word. Psalm 119:105 says that God's Word is a lamp unto your feet and a light unto your path. That path is the plan of God for your life, and the only way to walk it is to walk it by faith, one step, then another, and then another. Each one a step of faith in Jesus, and each laying a foundation for the next one. But if you've ever tried walking down a dark or dimly-lit path, then you know how difficult that can be. When you can't see what lies ahead or what dangers may be on the path, then you won't walk with confidence. This is precisely why Proverbs 4:18 says that the path of the just, or we might say, the plan of God for the life of the believer, is like the shining sun that's getting brighter and brighter. God's path gets brighter and brighter, but not so you can stand there and say, "Oh, look how pretty this path is." It's getting brighter so that you can see where you are going and walk boldly by faith down the road He's set you on. But without the Word of God there is no light, and without the light you are either standing still or stumbling in the dark—and neither one is God's plan for you.

God's Word is the most precious possession you have. Revelation from His Word is your way out of sin, sickness, depression, and lack, and it is your way into His good plan for your life. When He gave you Jesus, He gave you His Word made flesh. His Word is alive because Jesus is alive. His Word heals because Jesus heals. His Word saves because Jesus saves. But His Word cannot work in the life of someone who has no value for it. Just a few verses later, Proverbs 4 instructs us to give attention to and incline our ears to His Word, because they are life to those that find them and health to all their flesh. His words are life and health only to the ones who find them, value them, and keep them.

Fall in love with God's Word all over again, or for the first time. Simply meditate on the fact that He is meditating on you! Finding out what He thinks about you and about your future is simple, but you'll have to start with what He's already said about it in His Word. Spend time today with God in His Word, and let His Holy Spirit light up your path.

# JOURNAL

_____

_____

_____

_____

_____

_____

_____

_____

_____

_____

_____

_____

_____

_____

_____

_____

_____

_____

_____

_____

_____

_____

_____

_____

_____

_____

_____

_____

_____

_____

# 22

## KEEP YOUR GUARD UP

*"My son, give attention to my words; Incline your ear to my sayings. Do not let them depart from your eyes; Keep them in the midst of your heart; For they are life to those who find them, And health to all their flesh."*
**Proverbs 3:20-22 (NKJV)**

King Solomon left us a buried treasure in the book of Proverbs: thirty-one chapters of wealth and wisdom straight from God's heart. But to me there is one verse that stands out above the rest. Proverbs 4:23 begins with these three attention-gripping words: "Above everything else." Now we know that whatever words are about to follow this phrase must be extremely valuable and have the power to alter the course of our lives.

"Above everything else, guard your heart, because from it flow the springs of life" (Proverbs 4:23, NIV).

We have been not only encouraged but also commanded to guard our hearts. Why? Our lives depend on it. A guard has the responsibility to watch over, to make secure, and to protect from danger. Some people may passively skim over this verse and think, "Oh, that's nice and sounds easy enough." But take a closer look. Some translations say to guard your heart with diligence. A diligent guard is on duty at all times.

In this passage, Solomon is not referring to the physical heart, the organ that pumps blood throughout the body. He is talking about your core, the very essence of who you are.

The *AMPC* translation reads, "out of it flows the springs of life." God designed His healing spring to flow from Jesus to our physical bodies—through every vein and every organ—providing restoration to every cell. Jesus said that out of you should flow a river of living water. That cleansing, healing river will flow freely and unhindered unless there is a blockage or a break in that flow. You could call it heartbreak.

Sickness and disease are oftentimes a result of a breakdown in the heart. Many physical issues that show up on the outside start on the inside. They have a spiritual root, a hurt that led to a doubt, a doubt that led to wrong thinking and wrong believing. A break in the flow of life from the heart. Heartbreak is any form of hurt in you that hasn't been healed.

Before there was unforgiveness, someone broke your heart. Before bitterness or resentment, you experienced heartache. All soul sicknesses, including insecurity, bitterness, and rejection, are not just feelings; they are serious issues of the heart that can only be healed by an encounter with Jesus.

But how do we guard our hearts? Let's back up and read a few verses before this: "My son, give attention to my words; incline your ear to my sayings. Do not let them depart from your eyes; keep them in the midst of your heart; for they are life to those who find them, and health to all their flesh" (Prov. 4:20-22).

We keep our hearts by keeping the Word in our hearts. I want to encourage you to examine your heart today. Get honest with yourself and with God. If you need to forgive someone who has hurt you, make it your first priority. Forgiveness and healing flow from the same source. When you choose to forgive someone by faith, not based on your feelings, you open yourself up to the springs of life. Let go of every hurt holding you back and experience a rush of His love!

# *JOURNAL*

_____

_____

_____

_____

_____

_____

_____

_____

_____

_____

_____

_____

_____

_____

_____

_____

_____

_____

_____

_____

_____

_____

_____

_____

# 23

## LOVED BY LOVE

*"He who does not love does not know God, for God is love."*
*1 John 4:8 (NKJV)*

The person most dangerous and destructive to the kingdom of darkness is the born-again child of God who knows how much they're loved. There is no limit to what God can do for or through a believer who is totally convinced that God loves them. When you live with the revelation of how much God loves you, you're confident there's nothing He wouldn't do for you. But, when you live with the constant awareness of how much God loves others, then you know there's nothing He couldn't do *through* you.

Imagine that you are going about your day, minding your own business, when suddenly someone catches your attention. Maybe you notice they have a physical problem or challenge, or perhaps you recognize that same cloud of depression hanging over them that used to loom heavy over you. Whatever it is, and for whatever reason, you are being pulled in their direction. What's moving you towards them is the same compassion of God that moved Jesus towards the people He ministered to. Of course, it would be easy to resist the prompting you have to minister to them, thinking, *"What if I'm wrong or what if it's not God leading me? What if it's just me? I'll look like a fool if I go talk to that stranger."* Don't fight it, just do it! Besides, this is not about you or what they will think of you. This is about Love loving them *through* you. First John 4:18 says,

*"There is no fear in love; but perfect love casts out fear, because fear involves torment. But he who fears has not been made perfect in love."*

Imagine how differently you would live your life if you were totally free from fear. Imagine how confident and bold you would be at all times. You'd never again worry about what people think of you, because you'd know what Love thinks of you. You'd be free to say exactly what the Holy Spirit tells you to, because greater is He who is in you. And you'd go anywhere Love sent you, because you have no fear of death.

So why don't more Christians live like this? Because we don't yet believe how much Love loves us. If you're not "full" of the love of God, then you've been feeding at the wrong table. It's time you and I sat down at the table Love has prepared for us.

Dine on Love's grace. Feast on Love's mercy. Taste and see how good Love has been to you. Today's meal is being served from the book of 1 John, so come sit at the table and eat until you are stuffed full of the revelation of how much you are loved by Love. But save room for dessert from Romans 8! How sweet it is to know that if Love is for you, then no one can successfully be against you (verse 31). Ready for a big bite? Verses 35-39 say that you are more than conquerors through Him who loves you, and nothing can separate you from the love of God, which is in Christ Jesus our Lord! When you are *full* of love, you are free from fear!

# JOURNAL

_____
_____
_____
_____
_____
_____
_____
_____
_____
_____
_____
_____
_____
_____
_____
_____
_____
_____
_____
_____
_____
_____
_____
_____

# 24

## REST FOR YOUR SOUL

*"He makes me to lie down in green pastures; He leads me
beside the still waters. He restores my soul; He leads me in
the paths of righteousness For His name's sake."*
**Psalm 23:2-3 (NKJV)**

Not long after we started our ministry, the Lord spoke to Jeremy and me and told us to get healthy in our souls. We knew He wanted to give us more vision and expand our sphere of influence, but our increase was contingent on us becoming healthier.

Many may ask, "Well, then did you join a gym, hire a personal trainer, or adopt a new eating plan?" But that wasn't at all what God was dealing with us on. He wanted us to get completely healthy on the inside, strong and secure, joyful and confident, and completely anchored in His love.

During the healing process I realized that a soul at rest is a healthy soul. It took me a while to learn how to juggle ministry and motherhood. At times, I became overwhelmed trying to be a good wife, mommy, and minister. I let stress in as I tried to fulfill all my duties at home. I somehow managed to prepare for upcoming services while cleaning up diaper disasters and sorting through the piles of laundry that our suitcases had thrown up in our entryway.

Around the same time, Jeremy and I left our one-year-old with my mom over the weekend while we went to minister out of the country. When I came home, I scooped him up into my arms, and we began to cuddle. We turned the lights down, turned on the music, and danced around the room. Justus would lay his head on my shoulder and go completely limp in my arms. He was so calm and relaxed, following my lead as I carried and whirled him sweetly around the room. This particular night I was so thankful to hold him again that I whispered in his ear, "Buddy, these are my favorite moments with you." Immediately I heard the still, small voice of our Father God whisper inside me, "Sarah, these are My favorite moments with you, when you lay your head on My shoulder, rest, and let Me move."

The Psalmist writes, "He makes me to lie down in green pastures, He leads me beside the still waters, He restores my soul" (Psalm 23:2-3). I've been interested to learn that sheep by nature will not lie down and rest if they are hungry, stressed, nervous, or fearful. Have any of these symptoms kept you up past your bedtime—one thought after another, your soul spinning out of control? I have found that any issues with rest are really just issues of faith.

Hebrews 4:3-10 says, "For we who have believed do enter that rest... There remains therefore a rest for the people of God. For he who has entered His rest has himself also ceased from his works as God did from His."

You cannot separate faith and rest. When you're in faith, you're at rest. At times I've had to speak to my soul and declare over and over, "Grace is working, and I am resting."

Jesus said, "Come to Me, all you who labor and are heavy-laden and overburdened, and I will cause you to rest. [I will ease and relieve and refresh your souls]" (Matthew 11:28, AMPC). I want to encourage you to respond to His invitation and return to His presence. Come, enter into His rest and be refreshed.

# JOURNAL

_____

_____

_____

_____

_____

_____

_____

_____

_____

_____

_____

_____

_____

_____

_____

_____

_____

_____

_____

_____

_____

_____

_____

_____

# 25

## LIFT UP. LOOK FROM.

*"...Eye has not seen, nor ear heard, Nor have entered into the heart of man The things which God has prepared for those who love Him. But God has revealed them to us through His Spirit. For the Spirit searches all things, yes, the deep things of God." 1 Corinthians 2:9-10 (NKJV)*

*What's your name? Where do you live? What car do you drive? Where do you work? How much money do you have?*

You can answer every one of these questions with absolute certainty. You don't hesitate for even a moment because you are sure of who you are, where you live and work, and how much you have. Everyone is sure of what is "right now" because everything in the here and now can be seen and felt. But what would life be like if you had this same certainty regarding your future? "But I can't see my future." That's because you're not looking in the right place.

In Genesis 13:14-15, the Lord spoke to Abram after Lot had separated from him; and He said, "Lift your eyes now and look from the place where you are—northward, southward, eastward, and westward; for all the land which you see I give to you and your descendants forever." The Lord's instruction here is a simple two-step process. Step one: Lift up. Step two: Look from.

Abram was being given a front-row view to his future, but notice he was going to have to lift up his eyes and look from the place where he was. There was no way he was going to ever see what God had in store for him if his eyes were down and looking at the place where he was standing. The opposite of lifting up and looking from is letting down and looking at. And sadly, this is the condition most of the world and many Christians are living in—obsessed with their present positions and current conditions. Most people know exactly where they've been and where they are, but they have no idea where they are going. It's time we begin to look into our future.

I can tell you what is on God's mind right now, and it's not your past. He said that He knows the thoughts and plans that He thinks towards us (Jer. 29:11). So, obviously, He is thinking about the plan. Try as you may, you can't plan the past. Plans belong to the future. The operation of the Spirit of God in you is to reveal to you the things that God has prepared for those who love Him (I Cor. 2:9,10).

You'll never see the good things God has in store for you by being obsessed with where you are right now. "Let us run with endurance the race that is set before us, looking unto Jesus, the author and finisher of our faith" (Heb. 12:1,2). My friend, your future is in Jesus, and your life is hidden with Christ in God (Col. 3:3). Lift up your eyes and look at Jesus!

Have you ever wondered why we close our eyes when we pray? It's because we don't need them. As believers, we are not supposed to fix our eyes on the things that are seen. Those things are temporary. It's the unseen things that are eternal. Spend some time today with your eyes closed, looking at your future and at things that can't be seen.

# JOURNAL

_____

_____

_____

_____

_____

_____

_____

_____

_____

_____

_____

_____

_____

_____

_____

_____

_____

_____

_____

_____

_____

_____

_____

# 26

## SECRET PETITIONS

*"Delight yourself also in the Lord, And He shall give you the desires of your heart." Psalm 37:4 (NKJV)*

The *Amplified* translation of Psalm 37:4 says, "Delight yourself also in the Lord, and He will give you the desires and secret petitions of your heart." To make a petition is to request or to ask for something desired. To petition can also mean to press. I've learned that if I want God's best in my life, it won't just fall on me; I have to press for it. I have to go after it.

Pressing into God is not the same thing as putting pressure on people. I'm talking about possessing a kind of faith that presses into His presence, faith that presses into prayer, faith that presses into praise, and faith that presses into His plan. This kind of faith will press beyond its natural boundaries, lay hold of a promise with both hands, and refuse to let go. I'm talking about a living faith that draws a line in the sand and chooses to step over, pressing past what it's always seen and known, daring to believe there's something better.

For example, if you've come from a broken family, and all you've ever seen and all you've ever known is strife and divorce, and you want better, you must press into God and believe that He can and will give you a healthy home and a marriage made in heaven. If everyone in your family has been diagnosed with the same disease, you must press past your medical history and choose to trust that "the Lord will take away from you all sickness, and will afflict you with none of the terrible diseases… which you have known" (Deut. 7:15). If you've only ever lived from paycheck to paycheck, you have to imagine yourself stepping out of a dry land and over into wide-open pastures where the Good Shepherd is leading you and feeding you and bringing you into the best shape of your life. Real Bible faith is not rational and cannot be reasoned. Don't try to figure it out in your head. Choose to believe with your heart. You have to press for God's best.

A petition can also be a paper soliciting a favor, right, or mercy. Can you imagine God our Father in heaven sitting down to read the pile of petitions that clutter His desk every day? Sadly, He is unable to approve and answer so many prayers because they are full of doubt, worry, and unbelief; for we find in Hebrews 11:6 that "without faith it is impossible to please Him." But as He scans the stack, there are a few petitions full of faith that force Him to stop, command His attention, and bring a smile to His face. He moves his favorites to the top of the pile, not because He is a respecter of persons, but because He is a respecter of faith.

I believe one of the main reasons people do not receive their secret petitions is they have simply stopped enjoying the Lord and have started seeking things. Psalm 37:4 (ERV) says, "Enjoy serving the Lord, and He will give you whatever you ask for." In *The Living Bible*, it says, "Be delighted with the Lord. Then He will give you all your heart's desires." *The Message* says, "Keep company with God, get in on the best."

I want to encourage you today to delight big and dream big. Begin to enjoy Him again, and He will give you the secret petitions of your heart.

# JOURNAL

---
---
---
---
---
---
---
---
---
---
---
---
---
---
---
---
---
---
---
---
---
---
---
---
---
---
---

# 27

## WHO CARES?

*"Therefore I say to you, do not worry about your life..."*
*Matthew 6:25 (NKJV)*

*Who cares?* is a question we often ask but we don't often expect to be answered. I think it's a great question that needs to be answered in total confidence by every believer. 1 Peter 5:5-7 says,

*"God resists the proud, but gives grace to the humble.' Therefore humble yourselves under the mighty hand of God, that He may exalt you in due time, casting all your care upon Him, for He cares for you."*

Our God is in the grace-giving business, and not only does He give grace, according to James 4:6, "He gives more grace." God's grace is God's help (Heb. 4:16). God's grace is God's strength (2 Cor. 12:9). God's grace is God's presence with you and His favor on you (Ex. 33:12-14). God's grace is any gift that has come from Him to you through Jesus. That means wisdom, righteousness, sanctification, and redemption are yours by grace through faith (1 Cor. 1:30), because all of these came to us through Jesus. "Thanks be to God, who gives us the victory through our Lord Jesus Christ" (1 Cor. 15:57).

When you and I look around, we see an overwhelming majority of people living without His help, without His strength, and without a manifestation of His presence or favor in their lives. So we have to ask ourselves, "Who gets the grace?" According to Chapter 5 of 1 Peter, the humble get the grace. Let's think about the grace that came to us in salvation. You'd agree that we were saved by grace, wouldn't you? Then how did we get that grace? We humbled ourselves by saying, "Jesus, I make you Lord of my life. I've been my own lord, and look at the mess I've made of that. I'm done being lord, so I bow my knee to You." In exchange for humility, you got grace.

Here in 1 Peter 5:7, we see that we humble ourselves under the mighty hand of God by casting all our cares, our worries, our stress, and our anxious toil onto the One who cares for us. If the question is "Who cares?"; the answer is, "Jesus does."

In Matthew 6:25, Jesus was very clear with us along these lines. He said, "Therefore I say to you, do not worry about your life." I like those two little words *do not*. Look them up for yourself, and you'll find that they could have, and maybe even should have, been translated "Stop it!" When Jesus said, "Do not worry," He was telling us to stop worrying right now. Don't do it for another minute. Many people don't believe it's possible, but the truth is, you don't have to allow worry to rule you. You don't have to let anxious thoughts control your heart and mind. Of course those thoughts will come, but when they do, you just ask out loud, "Who cares? Who cares about my children? Who cares about my finances? Who cares about my health? Who cares about my job?" Then shout the answer, "Jesus does!"

It's pride that says, "I can carry this care on my own." But humility says, "Jesus, I'm not strong enough, but I know you are. I cast all my cares on You. Thank You for being my care-taker." If you'll do this every day, you can expect more and more of God's great grace in your life.

There is no fear in love, so meditate today on how deeply you are loved by Jesus. There can be no anxious, worried, or tormenting

thought that can remain in a heart that is persuaded of His perfect
love.

## *JOURNAL*

_____

_____

_____

_____

_____

_____

_____

_____

_____

_____

_____

_____

_____

_____

_____

_____

_____

_____

_____

_____

_____

_____

_____

_____

# 28

## STOP AND STARE

*"Now when they saw the boldness of Peter and John, and perceived that they were uneducated and untrained men, they marveled. And they realized that they had been with Jesus." Acts 4:13 (NKJV)*

It is impossible to stare at two different things at the same time. You cannot stare at your symptoms and stare at your Savior simultaneously and see results.

In Acts 3:4, we see a lame man in need of a miracle. Peter says to him, "Look at us," requiring his attention in order to be healed. Similarly, remember what Proverbs 4:20-22 urges us to do:

*My son, give attention to my words;*
*Incline your ear to my sayings.*
*Do not let them depart from your eyes;*
*Keep them in the midst of your heart;*
*For they are life to those who find them,*
*And health to all their flesh.*

Giving our attention to the Word will always produce healing in our souls and in our bodies.

The lame man in Acts 3 gave them his attention "expecting to receive something from them" (v. 5). Even though this man probably hoped to receive natural currency from them, this same principle applies to us spiritually: miracles still happen as a result of looking and expecting.

But many people do not have time to focus on Jesus because they live their lives on a racetrack, dashing through life without realizing it, filling up their days with too many activities, rushing to and from work, barely stopping to refuel on fast food because there's no time to enjoy a meal. They speed past their spouses and kids, not to mention Jesus standing on the sidelines, then reach the finish line for the day, only to start the stress cycle over again in the morning.

Because priorities are all out of whack, people spend the remainder of their time staring at Facebook™ and social media instead of spending quality time with their family and friends. It's no wonder so many are unhappy and sick, their marriages failing, and families falling apart. Many are crumbling under the pressure of the debt-and-death cycle, working their lives away and still have nothing to show for it.

As I meditated on these things, I heard the Lord speak this phrase to my heart, "If I can capture your stare, I can change your circumstance."

Whatever we spend the majority of our time looking at, we open ourselves up to. That's why I don't have the desire to watch homicide shows or medical dramas on television. Why would I spend an hour of my day staring at sickness and disease when I could spend that same time enjoying His peace in the presence of my Healer.

Nothing has the power to totally transform us like time spent staring at Jesus. After forty years as a crippled, hopeless beggar, the man at the gate called Beautiful had a moment with Jesus that changed his life forever. When he fixed his eyes on them, Jesus lifted him up and made something of him—a dancing miracle, who caused everyone around him to stand in awe of God. His testimony affected his street, his church, his city, and is now affecting the nations. When people marveled at Peter and John, trying to give them the credit for this man's healing, they pointed to Jesus and gave Him all the glory. People marveled when they realized that this miracle was all because Peter and John "had been with Jesus" (Acts 4:13).

## JOURNAL

---

---

---

---

---

---

---

---

---

---

---

---

---

---

---

---

---

# 29

## MAKE YOURSELF USEFUL

*"One who cleanses himself from these things will be a vessel for honor, sanctified, fit for the Master's use, and prepared for every good work." 2 Timothy 2:21 (MEV)*

2 Timothy 2:21 from the *Modern English Version* reads, "One who cleanses himself from these things will be a vessel for honor, sanctified, fit for the Master's use, and prepared for every good work." Here in this verse the word "fit" could also be translated "useful," and is used to describe someone who is in good shape or condition to be of some use to Jesus in His ministry. We never want to hear Jesus say, "I love you but I can't use you - not in the shape you're in."

You may think that sounds harsh and that surely Jesus would never say that to anyone He loves, but He would say it, because He did say it more than once. In Luke 9:59 Jesus said to someone, "Follow me." Those same two words had changed the lives of guys like Peter, Andrew, and the other disciples. When they heard them, they immediately dropped what they were doing and followed Him. But when this person in Luke 9:59 heard those words he replied, "Lord, let me first go and bury my father." "Let the dead bury their own dead," Jesus replied. "You go and preach."

We don't know much about this person; but we do know that he, just like all of us, was deeply loved by Jesus. We also know he was called by Jesus to be a part of His ministry team. But though this person was loved and called, still he didn't get used, simply because he wasn't ready to go when Jesus called. "Let me first..." he said. He didn't tell Jesus, "No." He just said there was something else he needed to do first. When there is still something else to do before you answer the Lord's call, then you're not in shape or ready to go. You're not as Paul put it to Timothy, "prepared for every good work."

In verse 61 Jesus offered the same invitation to another man who replied, "Lord, I will follow You, but let me first go and bid them farewell who are at my house." He too said, "Let me first..." They both said "me first," and if you know anything about living for the Lord, then you know it's not "me first" but rather "Kingdom first" in all things and at all times. Notice Jesus' response to these guys in verse 62. "No one having put his hand to the plow, and looking back, is fit for the kingdom of God." Again, the word "fit" means useful. Though Jesus loved and called both of these guys, they weren't ready, and because of that He said to them, "I can't use you. Not right now. Not in the shape you're in."

If you've heard the call of God on your life but you've told Him, "I will go Lord, but let me first save some money," or "let me first put the kids through school," or had any other priority, then you need to know that you're not yet fit to be used by Him. But the good news is you can get fit! Getting fit for Jesus isn't about getting physically stronger. He's not looking at the outward appearance. To see what kind of shape you're in, He looks at your heart; and if you'll tell Him right now that your heart belongs to Him, and that you are willing to go wherever, do whatever, and that nothing comes before Him, His Word, or His plan, then you are fit, in shape, and ready to go. You're not only someone He loves, you're someone He can use.

# *JOURNAL*

_____
_____
_____
_____
_____
_____
_____
_____
_____
_____
_____
_____
_____
_____
_____
_____
_____
_____
_____
_____
_____
_____
_____
_____
_____
_____
_____
_____

# 30

## THE GREAT ADVENTURE

*"This resurrection life you received from God is not a timid, grave-tending life. It's adventurously expectant, greeting God with a childlike "What's next, Papa?" God's Spirit touches our spirits and confirms who we really are. We know who he is, and we know who we are: Father and children. And we know we are going to get what's coming to us—an unbelievable inheritance!" Romans 8:15-16 (MSG)*

As a kid I craved adventure. There was nothing more exciting than following a handmade map to find a treasure buried deep in the back-yard. My brothers and I spent countless hours exploring the woods that surrounded our house, searching for bugs or rocks or anything exciting that forced us to venture out of the mundane and into the unknown. Two of our favorite movies were *The Goonies* and *Indiana Jones* because they kept us on the edge of our seats. Even as a society, we start out young playing games like hide-and-seek, going on egg hunts for Easter and scavenger hunts for birthday parties–all moving us to do what we were created for in the first place: to seek, to expect, and to find, as we long for the element of surprise. Why is that? Be-cause you want adventure. I want adventure. We all want adventure.

Adventure is in our blood because our Father is the great Adventurer. He lies awake at night thinking about us, planning His next exhila-rating paragraph in each of our tailor-made stories. As He writes His love-plan upon our hearts, we sense a stirring, begin to dream again, and realize that we were made for so much more. Romans 8:15-16 (MSG) says, "This resurrection life you received from God is not a timid, grave-tending life. It's adventurously expectant, greeting God with a childlike 'What's next, Papa?' God's Spirit touches our spirits and confirms who we really are. We know who He is, and we know who we are: Father and children. And we know we are going to get what's coming to us . . . inheritance!"

I love that it says our life should be "adventurously expectant" asking, "What's next, Papa?"

Stepping out in faith always requires taking a risk. The dictionary even describes adventure as a bold undertaking with unforeseen events. Many people never see their reward because they are afraid to take risks. But not us! One of my favorite authors, Lillian B. Yeomans, puts it like this, "God delights in his children stepping out over the aching void with nothing underneath their feet but the Word of God." Every day we should be listening for our next mission, ready to jump, fully expecting Him to catch us.

The Bible is our treasure map that leads us to what is truly valuable in life. The Holy Spirit is our torch, and if we'll hold on to Him, He'll light up our path and keep the fire burning. If we'll let Him, He'll take us on some of the most exciting adventures we could ever dream of. Yes, there may be a few snake pits to swing over, some crocs to kill, and some tigers to tame; but we'll also get to explore crystal-filled caves and travel through gold-laden tunnels and sail on oceans of His love. If we'll hold onto Him and let Him be our Guide, He will bring us safely through every valley; and at the end of our story, we'll still be standing on a mountaintop, strong and secure, heroes with hands lifted high to heaven giving all the glory to God.

I believe that people of faith have a spirit of adventure. They take risks when others play it safe, and they step out when God whispers, "Go!" They refuse to be bored but live life on the edge of their seats. They know His fire burning deep inside, and they let their hearts run wild.

I want to encourage you to go after God and seek His plan for your life. Get excited about your future, start expecting good things, and let the adventure begin!

# *J O U R N A L*

---

_____

_____

_____

_____

_____

_____

_____

_____

_____

_____

_____

_____

_____

_____

_____

_____

_____

_____

_____

# 31

## SATISFACTION GUARANTEED

*"I will satiate the soul of the priests with abundance,
And My people shall be satisfied with My goodness, says
the Lord." Jeremiah 31:14 (NKJV)*

Sarah and I had been ministering in Canada and were on our way home when we stopped in Wyoming to clear customs. The US Customs agent met us at the airplane and invited us to come into his office to fill out some paperwork so we could be on our way. He was a very friendly older man, and as he started on the paperwork, he pointed to the chairs we were sitting in. He told us that Mick Jagger and Keith Richards from The Rolling Stones had been sitting there just a week or two before.

He said Keith Richards sat right where we were sitting and told him about all the cocaine he'd done in his lifetime; how he'd spent millions and millions buying the purest cocaine in the world; and how he would fly on a regular basis to some remote place in Europe to have a total blood transfusion, just so he could do more cocaine without it killing him. "Really?" The customs agent replied. "And how much of it do you have on you right now?"

Keith was clean, and we laughed at the story; but before I get to the point I'm making, I want to draw your attention to Jeremiah 31:14: "I will satiate the souls of the priests with abundance, and My people shall be satisfied with My goodness, says the Lord."

It's no coincidence that The Rolling Stones got famous singing a song that said, "I try, and I try, and I try, but I can't get no satisfaction." They proved that satisfaction can't be found in massive amounts of cocaine, alcohol, money, or fame. Still, people are searching for satisfaction in these places, only to come to the end of their lives having found none. Many are resolved that satisfaction is a myth, a mirage, or a mystical fantasy that lives only in fairytales. But satisfaction is real and can indeed be found, you just have to know where to look. While the rest of this world clamors in futility to find satisfaction, it should be the Church that lives in the reality of the promise from God to satisfy His people with His goodness.

Psalm 27:13 says, *"I would have lost heart unless I had believed that I would see the goodness of the Lord in the land of the living."* Are you, like the Psalmist David, expecting to see the goodness of the Lord in your life? Though David was on the brink of losing heart and giving up because of the intense pressure and persecution, still there was something sustaining him and keeping him in the fight of faith. It was his constant expectation of seeing the goodness of God manifest in his life. If you're not satisfied when you look around and see that you're living a life that looks more like someone who doesn't have a covenant of salvation, healing, deliverance and prosperity with God, then let me ask you a question: "What were you expecting?"

You will never experience the goodness of God in your life until you begin confidently expecting to see it every day . Simply put, go back to the faith fundamentals of believing God's Word and declaring God's Word. Why not start with Jeremiah 31:14? Say over and over, "The Lord satiates my soul with abundance, and I am satisfied with His goodness!" Your expectation will soon make way for God's guaranteed satisfaction.

# JOURNAL

_____

_____

_____

_____

_____

_____

_____

_____

_____

_____

_____

_____

_____

_____

_____

_____

_____

_____

_____

_____

_____

_____

_____

_____

_____

_____

# 32

## THANKS A LOT

*"Therefore by Him let us continually offer the sacrifice of praise to God, that is, the fruit of our lips, giving thanks to His name." Hebrews 13:15 (NKJV)*

Each time I travel, I can't help but pick up a phrase or two from the cultures that I visit. My favorite would have to be two plain but incredibly powerful words: *Thank You.* In Mexico, they say, "Gracias." Some in South Africa say, "Dankie." In Israel and in Hebrew it's, "Toda." In Hawaii, "Mahalo," and in Australia, simply put, "Ta." But my favorite of all is how the British express their gratitude: "Cheers!" I think the reason I like it so much is because it just sounds so happy!

Real-Bible, God-pleasing faith lets out a happy sound. If we really knew the gift that God has given us in the person of Jesus, we would start every morning and end every night with a smile on our faces and a big, "Thank You, Father." When someone gives you a gift, as you reach out to take it, the appropriate response is always, "Thank you."

I am convinced that there is nothing more pleasing to God than a thankful heart. You might argue, "Well, I thought that the scriptures say that without faith it is impossible to please God. Isn't faith what pleases God the most?" My answer would be, Yes! You're exactly right, and that's exactly what I just said. Let me explain.

When I was a little girl, we lived out in the country next to a peach orchard. One of my favorite things to do was go on walks along its winding paths while picking peaches off of the trees. The fruit that hangs on any tree is the proof of what is happening inside that tree. If you see apples on a tree, you know that the seed that is causing the apples to grow is an apple seed deep within the core of that tree. It's the same with any kind of fruit. You can tell what is happening on the inside by what is showing up on the outside. Hebrews 13:15 says, "Therefore by Him let us continually offer the sacrifice of praise to God, that is, the fruit of our lips, giving thanks to His name."

Years ago, when I was preparing to minister on some of these things, the Lord spoke to my heart and said, "Thanksgiving is the language of faith." I see now that thanksgiving is the fruit, or the proof, that faith is working in the heart. If a *thank You* is on our lips, then we can be sure that faith is in our hearts.

I heard a true story about a professional athlete who had been diagnosed with a debilitating disease. He was about to lose his career before it had even started. In the hospital room he began to cry out to God, and, much to his surprise, he heard God speak back to him. He said, "Be more thankful." At first the man didn't understand how this could be the answer to his recovery and to his future success in life. But he obeyed and started thanking God in everything. Soon after, he began to recover. He's alive today, setting new records in his sport and living out his dream.

So even before you feel your healing, before you see your provision, or before you experience your breakthrough, be thankful; and remember that victory belongs to those who give thanks in the space between where they are and where they want to be.

# *JOURNAL*

---
---
---
---
---
---
---
---
---
---
---
---
---
---
---
---
---
---
---
---
---
---
---
---
---
---
---
---

# 33

## THINK AGAIN

*"For I know the plans and thoughts that I have for you,'*
*says the Lord, 'plans for peace and well-being and not for*
*disaster, to give you a future and a hope."*
*Jeremiah 29:11 (AMP)*

We can't be reminded enough that God is thinking about us. He's had us on His mind for a very long time, and when He's thinking about you, He's thinking about your future—not your past. You can't plan the past, and no one knows this better than God. You'll never experience God's future while trying to maintain a relentless grasp on the past. Let it go!

It's time for us to get on the same page with God, and when you are constantly lamenting over things that happened yesterday, last week, or 25 years ago, you are trying to have a conversation with God that He's not interested in having. In fact, if you have received your forgiveness, then God really has no idea what you are talking about. It's time for us to find out what's been on His mind, then exchange our thoughts for His thoughts (Colossians 3:2, Romans 8:5-6).

Thinking God's thoughts will connect you to life. Anything else connects you to death. You can see now why God was more than a little upset in Jeremiah 29. There were so-called prophets and diviners speaking on His behalf that were not from Him. He finally had to speak up through Jeremiah and say, "Don't listen to these people! They don't know what I think because I haven't told them what I think. I know what I think, and if you want to know My thoughts, you're going to have to listen to Me!"

Maybe you're reading this saying, "Yeah, but I never hear God speak to me." If that's you, then stop staying that! Open your Bible and read. You have in your hand His thoughts, His words, and the revelation of His will. You are literally holding your future. Not only has He given you His Word, He has also given you His Spirit. How are you going to know and walk in the plan God has for your life? By being led by His Spirit (1 Corinthians 2:9-12).

God has revealed to us by His Spirit the things that He has prepared for us. Once again, you can't prepare for the past. Preparation is for the future. And the only way we are going to know what God has prepared for our future is by listening to and following the leading of the Spirit.

Thank God, He put His Spirit in us, and we can know His thoughts. Jesus, our example, didn't say or do anything without hearing from His Father first. Jesus was on the same page with God at all times, and He did it that way to show us that we can be, too. 1 Corinthians 2:16 goes on to say, "We have the mind of Christ." You and I were created with the capacity to think God's thoughts. Dig into His Word and allow His Spirit to reveal to you the brilliant future He's been preparing for you all this time.

# JOURNAL

_____

_____

_____

_____

_____

_____

_____

_____

_____

_____

_____

_____

_____

_____

_____

_____

_____

_____

_____

_____

_____

_____

_____

_____

_____

# 34

## THE LOVING-KINDNESS
## OF THE LORD

*"Who redeems your life from destruction, Who crowns you*
*with lovingkindness and tender mercies..."*
**Psalm 103:4 (NKJV)**

Many people in the world and in the church are confused about God. They are unsure if He is hard and harsh, or warm and welcoming. They wonder if He is angry or caring, not totally convinced that He is good all the time. They may not say it out loud, but for some this question lingers deep in their hearts: *"Is He cruel, or is He kind?"*

In the book of Ruth, we meet Naomi who has been overcome with grief after losing her husband and two sons. The sorrow in her soul leads to confusion about God's true nature. She tells her daughters-in-law to return home to their families, and she cries out, "The hand of the Lord has gone out against me!" (Ruth 1:13).

She lets her circumstances and other people tell her who God is. But is God really against her? Or is she just confused about His character?

How we see God and how we think He sees us will affect every area of our lives.

When Naomi and her daughter-in-law Ruth return to Bethlehem, Ruth finds favor while gleaning in a field owned by a rich man named Boaz. As she gleans behind the reapers, He takes notice of her and begins to show her overwhelming kindness, even though she is a poor foreigner. He becomes a refuge and protects her by commanding the young men not to touch her. He makes sure she has water to drink while she works. He comforts her with his words and speaks kindly to her. How romantic! He tells the other workers not to shame her and to let extra grain "fall purposely for her" (Ruth 2:16). Ruth has more than enough food to eat until she is satisfied and has plenty to take home for Naomi.

For the first time in her life, Naomi encounters kindness through Boaz, and it radically changes her perspective of God forever. She rejoices, "Blessed be he of the Lord, who has not forsaken His kindness to the living and the dead!" (Ruth 2:20). Naomi is able to see the true kindness of God only after she comes face to face with the one who would become her kinsman-redeemer.

It is only in the face of Jesus, our Redeemer, that we are able to clearly see the kindness of our Father God.

Ruth is so swept away with Boaz's kindness towards her that she finds enough boldness to lie down at his feet while he is sleeping, and then she makes a huge request. She asks him to take her under his wing and become her kinsman-redeemer (Ruth 3:7-9). To the Hebrew, to take someone under your wing is a big deal. It is to become an unconditional caretaker. It is an extreme expression of intimacy. Boaz becomes her kinsman-redeemer by marrying her, and he selflessly uses his wealth to buy back Naomi's inheritance, restore her family, rescue them from danger, and provide for all their needs. In a sense, he crowns them with his "loving-kindness and tender mercies" (Psalm 103:4) and gives them a status beyond what they deserve.

See, God was good to Naomi all along. He was always kind. He had a beautiful plan prepared for her. She just didn't know it. She couldn't see Him clearly. Her confusion is understandable because when she looked at God, there was a veil between them: "But when the kindness and the love of God our Savior toward man appeared" (Titus 3:4), our eyes became wide open. Jesus shined the light on God's character, and now we can see Him for who He really is—eternally and relentlessly kind.

## JOURNAL

_____

_____

_____

_____

_____

_____

_____

_____

_____

_____

_____

_____

_____

_____

_____

_____

_____

_____

# 35

## WE'RE RICH!

*"The law of Your mouth is better to me Than thousands of coins of gold and silver." Psalm 119:72 (NKJV)*

I once read about a man in *Time Magazine* that found a collection of old baseball cards while cleaning out the attic in his late aunt's home. Focused solely on the work still to be done on the house, he set the box of cards aside, and went back to packing and cleaning. It wasn't until two weeks later that he opened the box to take a closer look and recognized some of the players as Hall of Famers from as far back as the early 1900s. Not only were the players famous, but the cards themselves had somehow been preserved in perfect mint condition. He had a hunch they might have been worth something. He was right. The collection was authenticated by memorabilia experts and immediately given a value of $3 million. It has been called the greatest sports memorabilia find in history, and the one to which all other collections would be compared.

What would your response have been if you had been the one to find a three-million-dollar box of baseball cards? My guess is that after you regained consciousness you would probably get very, very excited. Do you know that we ought to have this same kind of excitement about the Word of God? David said in Psalm 119:162, "I rejoice at Your word as one who finds great treasure."

The Bibles belonging to many Christians are a lot like that box of baseball cards. Inside is a life changing treasure - a wealth beyond all we could ask or think. But sadly, many Bibles all over the world sit on a shelf just like that box did, unopened and ignored for weeks at a time. But when you open the Word of God, you're opening a treasure box worth more than all the gold and silver in the world. David knew this and that's why he said in Psalm 119:14, "I have rejoiced in the way of your testimonies as much as in all riches." Later, in verse 72, he said, "The law of Your mouth is better to me than thousands of coins of gold and silver." I can hear the excitement in his voice when he exclaimed in verse 127, "Therefore I love your commandments more than gold, yes, than fine gold!" God's testimonies, His law, and His commandments are all synonyms for His Word; and I think it's time we ask ourselves if we, too, feel the same way David did about the Word of God. If you've lost your love for the scriptures, then simply ask the Holy Spirit to help you rekindle your passion, desire, and hunger for God's Word.

In this 119th Psalm, David also said to the Lord, "Turn away my eyes from looking at worthless things, and revive me in Your words." (verse 37) If you'll pray that same thing in faith, God will begin to stir in your heart a renewed passion and desire for time with Him in His Word; and the Holy Spirit will give you eyes to see what is truly valuable in this life, and what is a worthless waste of your time.

I pray today that you will begin to experience the thrill of revelation from the Word of God. I pray that as you open His Word and enter into conversation with Jesus, the Word made flesh, that you realize how truly rich you really are.

# JOURNAL

_____

_____

_____

_____

_____

_____

_____

_____

_____

_____

_____

_____

_____

_____

_____

_____

_____

_____

_____

_____

_____

_____

_____

_____

_____

_____

_____

_____

# 36

## THE FAITH FREQUENCY

*"But without faith it is impossible to please Him, for he
who comes to God must believe that He is, and that He is a
rewarder of those who diligently seek Him."*
*Hebrews 11:6 (NKJV)*

In high school and college, I worked as a deejay at a Christian radio station owned by my church. I so clearly remember sitting at my
desk with my oversized headphones speaking to our radio audience:
"You're listening to KMTC 91.1 FM—Keeping you More than a Con-
queror."

At the top of every hour, I announced the time and played the nation-
al news, then gave the local weather forecast for the River Valley. In
those old-school radio days, nothing was done on computer, so part
of my job was to scan the wall of Christian albums for the perfect
songs to minister to our listeners. At that time, KMTC was the only
Christian radio station that you could pick up in our town, and it was
one of the only stations in all of Arkansas that played faith-filled music and teaching from the Word of God. Radio frequencies on either
side of ours were nothing but static, so if you wanted to hear what we
were playing, you had to tune in to the exact FM frequency—91.1.

Do you know that faith is a frequency? It is only by faith that we tune
in to God and He tunes into us. There is only one station that He
broadcasts from, and only one way we send out a signal to Him—
through the faith frequency. It is the only wavelength that He rides
on. Hebrews 11:6 says, "Without faith it is impossible to please Him,

for he who comes to God must believe that He is, and that He is a rewarder of those who diligently seek Him."

Without faith it is impossible to please God. What a huge statement that is! And nothing pleases the Father more than to bless His children. But if we want to receive anything from God, we must pray on the faith frequency, worship on the faith frequency, and live every moment of our lives on the faith frequency. If we want to dial into God, we have to tune in to only one frequency and tune everything else out. James 1:5-8 tells us how to do this: "If any of you lacks wisdom, let him ask of God, who gives to all liberally and without reproach, and it will be given to him. But let him ask in faith, with no doubting, for he who doubts is like a wave of the sea driven and tossed by the wind. For let not that man suppose that he will receive anything from the Lord; he is a double-minded man, unstable in all his ways."

We're not the only ones tuning in to the faith frequency. There's Someone else out there seeking and scanning the world over to find somebody who believes in Him and who will take Him at His Word. As a teenager, I was fascinated by my friend's police scanner that could pick up all kinds of frequencies. We would scan and scan until we found something interesting enough to capture our attention. In much the same way, "The eyes of the Lord run to and fro throughout the whole earth, to show Himself strong on behalf of those whose heart is loyal to Him" (2 Chron. 16:9). *The Common English Bible* translation says, "The Lord's eyes scan the whole world." God is scanning for faith. He scans until He hears us on the faith frequency. Faith is so captivating that it causes Him to stop in His tracks, tune His ear to our prayer, and go to work in our lives.

You don't have to spend another day trying to hear God through the static and noise. Tune your heart to the faith frequency, and you'll hear Him coming through loud and clear.

# *JOURNAL*

_____
_____
_____
_____
_____
_____
_____
_____
_____
_____
_____
_____
_____
_____
_____
_____
_____
_____
_____
_____
_____
_____
_____
_____

# 37

## ALL THE HELP YOU CAN GET

*"But He gives more grace." James 4:6 (NKJV)*

You ought to make James 4:6 your answer to every challenge you face today, this week, this year, and for the rest of your life. They say, "The kids are sick"; you say, "But He gives more grace." They say, "The economy is failing"; you say, "But He gives more grace." They say, "Our schools aren't safe anymore"; you say, "But He gives more grace!" This is good news, and you need to hear yourself say it often.

We know He gives more grace, but we have to find out just to whom exactly He's giving more grace. The rest of James 4:6 goes on to say, *"Therefore He says: 'God resists the proud, but gives grace to the humble.'"*

This is a quote from Proverbs 3:34 that is repeated again by Peter just a couple of pages later in your Bible:

*"Be clothed with humility, for 'God resists the proud, but gives grace to the humble.' Therefore humble yourselves under the mighty hand of God, that He may exalt you in due time,"*

*1 Peter 5:5-6*

God's grace is God's help. It is His involvement in your life that results in you being blessed in everything you set your hand to. But notice:

there is a comma, not a period, at the end of verse six. Verses 5 and 6 are the *why* and the *what*, but verse 7 is the *how*. How do you humble yourself to get more grace? By "casting all your care upon Him, for He cares for you." You are going to receive grace upon grace if you will humble yourself by casting your cares upon Jesus.

If casting your care is humility, then what is carrying your care? You guessed it. It's pride. The proud get resisted, which means they don't get the help. Let's say you offer your help and expertise to an individual who very obviously needs it, but instead of receiving it and stepping out of the way, he or she looks at you and says, "No, I got this." (This is Pride's motto.) Instead of casting their cares onto someone capable of handling them, they choose to make even bigger messes of them all. The only reason they don't have anyone helping them is because they refused the help when it was offered.

Don't refuse God's help! Quit telling Him that you got this. Cast the care, the worry, and the stress over on the One who cares for you - the One and only One capable of handling the care.

Make a quality decision that you'll gladly take all the help God is offering, even when it comes through the people around you. Begin to refuse every care and anxious thought. Say out loud, "That's not my thought! I cast my cares on the One who cares for me, the One who loves me and gave Himself for me! Jesus, You got this!"

# JOURNAL

_____
_____
_____
_____
_____
_____
_____
_____
_____
_____
_____
_____
_____
_____
_____
_____
_____
_____
_____
_____
_____
_____
_____
_____
_____
_____

# 38

## SONGS OF DELIVERANCE

*"You are my hiding place; You shall preserve me from
trouble; You shall surround me with songs of deliverance."*
**Psalm 32:7 (NKJV)**

Of all the amazing things that I've ever discovered about God, one of
my favorites is that He sings. He is not only a recipient of our worship
and our singing, He Himself sings over us! Zephaniah 3:17 in the
*World English Bible* says, "Yahweh, your God, is among you, a mighty
one who will save. He will rejoice over you with joy. He will calm you
in his love. He will rejoice over you with singing."

As a songwriter, I've found that you can't just sit down and crank
out a hit song from your head. A good song has to come straight
from the heart. What makes a song great is not only the words and
the melodies but the heart behind the words. Every song that God
sings over us comes straight from His heart, and we not only need
to hear His Word, but we need to sense His love that burns for us
in His Word. God's songs are not depressing or lackluster, but they
are like a wildfire-burning love that is hard to extinguish—spreading
swiftly across the surface of our lives. His voice is sweet to the hearer,
and His sound brings rest to the soul. God's songs will never drag
you down but always fuel your faith. They will never wear you out or
sound like defeat. When Jesus sings, you will always hear a tone of
triumph and victory in His voice.

During a time that my mom was standing in faith and believing for her healing after she had been given only 10 months to live, she said every morning she would wake up with a new song playing over and over in her head. After about a week of this, she realized that it wasn't just her subconscious looping a song she had heard the day before on the radio. These songs were not coming out of nowhere; they were coming from somewhere or better yet Someone. They were coming up from her spirit to help her overcome. When she told me this story, I remembered that scripture from Zephaniah, and I could see in the Spirit what was happening: God Himself was singing over her, and she was hearing His song! He was singing songs of healing and deliverance over her.

A really good love song doesn't just say *I love you*; it communicates a message from the heart. God was not only trying to sing a sweet love song over her, He was trying to get a message of healing to her. If she would just take His song and make it her own, things would begin to change. She did, and she is alive today, healthier than ever before.

So the next time you wake up in the middle of the night and a song full of the Word comes to your mind, don't be quick to dismiss it. See your Father strumming the strings of your heart, and hear Him serenading you with His songs of salvation. When you stare at Scripture, hear His love song to you. When you hear Him singing, don't just listen; join in the chorus. Life and death are in the power of your tongue. Find your harmony part and sing with Him! Then wait on Him in the secret place of His presence, and watch and listen as He surrounds you "with songs of deliverance" (Psalm 32:7).

# JOURNAL

_____
_____
_____
_____
_____
_____
_____
_____
_____
_____
_____
_____
_____
_____
_____
_____
_____
_____
_____
_____
_____
_____
_____
_____
_____

# 39

## ADJUST YOUR CLOCK

*"...do not become sluggish, but imitate those who through faith and patience inherit the promises."*
*Hebrews 6:12 (NKJV)*

Just days after our wedding, Sarah and I began traveling together full-time, ministering in churches and conferences around the world. We quickly got accustomed to adjusting our watches from one time zone to another, then back again on our way home. It would've been foolish for me to arrive in a faraway country and refuse to change my watch to the local time. "Why should I have to change *my* watch? I want to stay on *my* time from *my* hometown." There'd be no way to get anything accomplished without adjusting my clock, because I wouldn't be in cooperation with anyone or anything else in that city.

When you and I were born again, we moved out of darkness and into light—the kingdom of God. And if we are going to get anything done or receive anything from Him in His kingdom, then one of the first things we are going to have to do is adjust our clocks. Of course, I'm not talking about adjusting the timepiece on your wrist, your nightstand, or your oven. I'm talking about the one in your soul.

James 1:2-4 says, "My brethren, count it all joy when you fall into various trials, knowing that the testing of your faith produces patience. But let patience have its perfect work, that you may be perfect and complete, lacking nothing."

"Joy" is not the normal, natural response to trials and tests. Where does the smile on your face come from in the midst of trials and adverse circumstances that would cause most people to give up and quit? Genuine joy in the middle of a trial is the result of knowing something that most people don't know: your joy comes from knowing that patience is at work in you, and that you come out on the other end of this thing perfect, complete, and lacking nothing. Have you ever stopped long enough to allow the Holy Spirit to create an image in you of what life would look like if you were perfect, complete, and lacking nothing? If you believed that's the life you were headed for, then joy would be your supernatural response.

But look again at where this joy comes from: it comes from letting patience go to work in you. But patience isn't *just* about waiting a long time for something you want right now. While there is an element of waiting that is involved, patience is more about the condition in which you wait. Patience is defined as "cheerful endurance."

The truth is, you are now on Kingdom Standard Time, and you need to adjust your clock. Patience is learning to live on God's clock. As ridiculous as it would be for me to travel into another time zone and demand that everyone adjust their clocks to mine, it's even more foolish for a Christian to get frustrated with God and demand that He adjust His timing to theirs.

Hebrews 10:36 (NMB) says, "For you have need of patience." Question: if the Bible says you need patience, what do you need? Patience. We have to stop thinking that patience is something you're either born with or without; or that it's just a virtue that you weren't blessed to possess. Wrong. Patience is endurance. It is the God-given, Spirit-infused, refusal to quit believing. And why do we need it? Because through faith and patience, we inherit the promises (Heb. 6:12). Faith is believing. Patience is continuing to believe. The next time you feel that you have been waiting for God too long, and you feel like throwing in the towel, just reach down and adjust your clock. You're on His time zone now.

## JOURNAL

_____

_____

_____

_____

_____

_____

_____

_____

_____

_____

_____

_____

_____

_____

_____

_____

_____

_____

_____

_____

_____

_____

# 40

## THE UNBROKEN HEART

*"Now hope does not disappoint, because the love of God has been poured out in our hearts by the Holy Spirit who was given to us." Romans 5:5 (NKJV)*

A friend of mine was diagnosed with non-Hodgkin lymphoma at the young age of twenty-three. The doctors told her that there was a mass wrapped around her heart. She could barely breathe. It was literally suffocating her. I asked her about the years leading up to the diagnosis, and she expressed to me that they were full of hurt and heartbreak. When she was fifteen years old, her parents went through a traumatic divorce, and her life as a teenager was never peaceful again. Growing up, she was always very close to her father; but as the years went on, he slowly began to resent her with no explanation why. He became verbally abusive, and when she moved away to college at age eighteen, she sought help through many counselors in an effort to make sense of it all. Her soul stayed in a constant state of turmoil, trying to figure out why her father, who had always loved her, suddenly despised her.

She used two words to describe the five years leading up to the cancer: *heartbroken* and *rejected*. But several weeks into the treatment, she had a life-altering moment when she heard the Lord say to her, "I'm healing your heart, so I can heal your heart."

She said in that moment, all of the heaviness completely lifted from her, and she hasn't shed a tear over that situation since. She has been cancer free for at least a decade now, enjoying life and her ministry with her husband and family. Jesus had to heal the condition of her heart before He could heal her heart condition.

We can all learn from my friend's story that thoughts of rejection, feeling unloved, unwanted, unvalued, or never good enough are dangerous heart conditions and must not be left to linger. When you know the truth, the truth will set you free; and the truth is, "you are the ones chosen by God, chosen for the high calling of priestly work, chosen to be a holy people, God's instruments to do his work and speak out for him, to tell others of the night-and-day difference He made for you—from nothing to something, from rejected to accepted" (1 Peter 2:9, MSG).

Let's face the facts: if you haven't already, you will one day encounter rejection; but you're in good company! Jesus did too. Isaiah 53:3 says Jesus "[was] despised and rejected of men; a man of sorrows and acquainted with grief."

But keep reading; it gets good. "Surely He has borne our grief, and carried our sorrows" (Isa. 53:4). If you look up the word *grief*, you'll find that it can also mean heartache or heartbreak. Jesus' heart was broken so that yours wouldn't have to be!

Jesus revealed the assignment on His life when He found Himself in the pages of Scripture, stood up, and declared, "The Spirit of the Lord is upon Me because He has anointed Me… to heal the brokenhearted" (Luke 4:18). The health of your heart is a big deal to God, and you don't have to live another day with a broken heart. Pray this with me:

"Lord, I open my heart and make it tender before You now. I receive Your love washing over me, healing every hurt. I choose to forgive those who have hurt me. I receive Your love shed abroad in my heart by the Holy Spirit (Romans 5:5), filling the height, the width, the length, and the depth of my heart. Your perfect love is forcing fear out of me (1 John 4:18) and I am anchored and secure in You."

## *JOURNAL*

_____

_____

_____

_____

_____

_____

_____

_____

_____

_____

_____

_____

_____

_____

_____

_____

_____

_____

_____

_____

# 41

## TRUST ISSUES

*"Trust in the Lord with all your heart, And lean not on your own understanding..." Proverbs 3:5 (NKJV)*

I get so excited every time I think about the potential impact that can occur when money is put into the hands of people that know what God wants done with it! For several generations now the revelation of God's will to prosper His people has been preached. While there are some people that have experienced the prosperity that accompanies The Blessing of the Lord, still there are many that have heard the message but have yet to see it in their lives like God wants them to. The more I seek the Lord along these lines, the more I realize that our prosperity is contingent upon our ability to answer two simple questions:

1. Can you trust Him *for* it?
2. Can He trust you *with* it?

When it comes to prosperity, the Church has some real trust issues that need to be dealt with. Let's look at what Proverbs 3:5 instructs you to do: "Trust in the Lord with all your heart, and lean not on your own understanding." According to this verse, trusting God is diametrically opposed to trusting yourself, leaning on your own understanding. How were you born again? Did you earn it? Did you "figure out" salvation with your brilliant intellect? No! You put faith in the finished work of Jesus by believing in your heart and confessing with your mouth. You trusted God and His grace to save you, not yourself or your good works. You were filled with the Holy Spirit the same way, by asking, believing, and receiving. Outside of it requiring your faith, you had nothing to do with it! The same goes for the healing of your body, the gifts of the Spirit, or any other good thing that comes from God. If we know all this to be true, then why have we drawn the line when it comes to prosperity? Why do we feel like our increase is up to us?

God put it pretty plainly when He spoke through His prophet and said, "Cursed is the man who trusts in man and makes flesh his strength, whose heart departs from the Lord" (Jeremiah 17:5). Trusting in man to be your strength would include you trusting yourself or you putting trust in another person to be your strength and supply. But He went on to say in verse seven, "Blessed is the man who trusts in the Lord, and whose hope is the Lord." God has your financial increase ready and available, but before He can get it to you, He's asking you, "Can you trust Me for it, or will you continue to see yourself or others as your source?"

Trusting God as your one and only source is the first step to positioning yourself to receive the increase He wants you to have and the prosperity that Jesus paid for you to receive. Trusting is paramount to resting, and if you'll go back to Proverbs 3:5 you'll see that trusting is done with the heart. The healthiest Christians are those whose hearts are at rest, even in tight times, knowing that their God shall supply all their need according to His riches in glory by Christ Jesus. Make the decision today that you are going to trust God alone to be your source and supply for all the wisdom you need to increase materially and financially. When you get this trust issue resolved, you open the door to God's willingness and ability to bless you in every area of your life.

# JOURNAL

_____

_____

_____

_____

_____

_____

_____

_____

_____

_____

_____

_____

_____

_____

_____

_____

_____

_____

_____

_____

_____

_____

_____

# 42

## LET'S EAT!

*"You prepare a table before me in the presence of my enemies..." Psalm 23:5 (NKJV)*

Jesus is the only person who can satisfy and still leave you hungry for more. Psalm 107:9 (NIV) says, "For He satisfies the thirsty and fills the hungry with good things."

He is the Master Chef. He has spent all of His time in the kitchen preparing the perfect meal for you. In fact, He slaved over it: took stripes just for you, went to the cross just for you, laid down His life just for you. He did all the work! Now He rings the dinner bell and shouts, "It is finished! Come and get it!"

Now, there sits before you a dish full of healing, a pitcher of joy, a plate of peace, a platter of protection and prosperity. Will you come and eat? Grace sets the table. Faith eats!

Although the table has been set with plenty on it to appease your appetite, God will never force you to eat. In His grace, He will bring you to His banqueting table, but you still have to eat by faith. It is easier said than done. In Luke 14:16-18 (GNT), Jesus tells the parable of one great dinner: "There was once a man who was giving a great feast to which he invited many people. When it was time for the feast, he sent his servant to tell his guests, 'Come, everything is ready!' But they all began, one after another, to make excuses."

If you read on, you will find that all of the excuses seemed like pretty legitimate reasons not to show up for dinner. But Jesus didn't accept any of them. He summed the story up with this, "I tell you all that none of those who were invited will taste my dinner!" (Luke 14:24, GNT).

I refuse to miss out on the feast Jesus has set before me. I want everything He came to give me! The Lord gave us a verse to a song that says:

I will sit at the table you've prepared for me, Here I am safe from the enemy. I will feast on Your love and Your mercy, For death has lost its hold on me!

Psalm 23:5 says that He has prepared a table for you even in the presence of your enemies here on earth. That means even in the midst of fear or doubt, even in the presence of people who are against you, even in toughest times, you have a safe place to go. Sit down at His table and enter into His rest. Real faith rests in God. Take a good look at everything Grace has set on the table. See the spread that He has set before you and recall all that He has done for you. Grace has set the table. Faith eats everything on the plate. Come and find your seat. It's dinnertime, let's eat!

# *JOURNAL*

---
---
---
---
---
---
---
---
---
---
---
---
---
---
---
---
---
---
---
---
---
---
---
---

# 43

## SO LOVED

*"And we have known and believed the love that God has for us. God is love, and he who abides in love abides in God, and God in him." 1 John 4:16 (NKJV)*

Imagine you are driving on a road you've driven a thousand times before. You think you've got every inch of this road memorized; but on this day, you notice something on the side—a building, a tree, or a sign—and you say to yourself, "I've driven this road every day for years, yet I have never seen that before." You're seeing for the first time something that has been there all along. I wonder how many times we've broken the speed-reading limit blowing through familiar verses like John 3:16 and thinking there's nothing we haven't already seen. Let's slow down today and take a closer look:

*"For God so loved the world that He gave His only begotten Son, that whoever believes in Him should not perish but have everlasting life."*

I want you to notice a word here that you may not have ever noticed before. It's the word *so*. The shortest word in this verse packs a bigger punch than you might have realized. *So* is a word we use to express extent or degree: "I am *so* hungry!" "That guy is *so* tall!" "It is *so* hot in Texas!" This tiny word does something big in the understanding of the one speaking and the one listening.

My friends, you and I are not just loved—we are *so* loved. I want you to hear Jesus saying these words to you, and I want you to understand them in the way He is saying them. He wants us living with the revelation that we are *so* loved by the Father.

Here's what's interesting about the word *so*. It is usually followed by the word *that*. Look again at verse sixteen, "For God so loved the world that He gave his only begotten Son." Again, the word *so* expresses the extent to which God loves us. But the word *that* is the proof that backs up *so*. In other words, God didn't just tell you *that* He loves you; He proved it by giving you Jesus.

First John 4:9 says, "In this the love of God was manifested toward us, that God has sent His only begotten Son into the world, that we might live through Him." The word *manifest* means to render apparent. God openly proved His love for you when He gave you the very best that He had to give.

I want you to think about it like this: Jesus was the only thing God could give you that would cost Him something. Jesus was the only thing God had just one of. And giving you Jesus didn't cost God *something*—it cost Him *everything*. That's what makes Jesus such a precious gift.

First John 4 goes on to say in verse sixteen that "we have known and believed the love that God has for us." What does it mean to "believe in Jesus"? To believe in Jesus is to believe how much you are loved. Faith works by love (Gal. 5:6). If you want your faith to soar to new heights, spend some time today meditating on how much you are loved by the Father. Your faith will work when you get a revelation of just how much you are loved.

# JOURNAL

_____

_____

_____

_____

_____

_____

_____

_____

_____

_____

_____

_____

_____

_____

_____

_____

_____

_____

_____

_____

_____

_____

_____

_____

_____

# 44

## TUNE YOUR HEART TO HEAR

*"Enter into His gates with thanksgiving, And into His courts with praise. Be thankful to Him, and bless His name." Psalm 100:4 (NKJV)*

How do you "tune in" to God? If you want to pick up a good signal, you have to have a good antenna. I'll never forget as a kid watching my dad work so hard to finagle the two tall metal rods into perfect position so that he could tune in to hear the basketball game. We lived out in the country, and if we wanted to pick up anything at all on TV, we had to do the same thing with that antenna. It seemed like such an ordeal, but if we adjusted our antenna just right by propping it up on some books, tilting it on its side, squinting one eye, and biting our lip, all of a sudden something magical began to happen! The static started to disappear as the picture and sound became loud and clear.

An antenna is sometimes called a receiver because it extends out to catch radio waves that are traveling at the speed of light. Your heart is your antenna. With your heart you can reach out to God, tune into His power, and receive all that He has for you. Sometimes it just takes making a few heart adjustments in order for the signal to come through loud and clear.

Here are three characteristics of a heart that hears clearly and receives freely. First is a thankful heart. Psalm 100:4 tells us to "enter into his gates with thanksgiving, and into his courts with praise." A way to "tune out" is to do the opposite—murmur and complain. Thanksgiving is the language of faith and faith is the only language that God speaks. If we want to have effective communication we must learn to speak His language.

Second it takes a genuine heart to connect with Him. Jesus teaches us what real worship is in John 4:23-24 (MSG): "Your worship must engage your spirit in the pursuit of truth. That's the kind of people the Father is out looking for; those who are simply and honestly themselves before him in their worship. God is sheer being itself—Spirit. Those who worship him must do it out of their very being, their spirits, their true selves..."

Real worship is putting away anything in us that is fake or false and getting real with Him. He's just waiting for us to start up a normal conversation like we would with a friend. It doesn't take kooky talk and hocus-pocus to conjure up something. It takes simple genuine faith to hang with Him. When we stop pretending, we start receiving.

Third is a willing heart. Jesus has a heart like this. In the garden, His flesh didn't want to go to the cross, but His spirit cried out to our Father, "Nevertheless, Thy will be done."

Before having our second baby, we began looking in Colorado for a new house to accommodate our growing family. Even after praying for wisdom, I couldn't get a witness on anything. The more we looked, the more frustrated we became. One night I opened my heart and cried out, "Lord, Your will be done!" Just as soon as I did, I knew the answer. With the eyes of my heart I saw a specific house that our friends were moving out of in a neighborhood in Fort Worth, Texas. I had never thought of living in that house before. We were looking in the wrong state! I realized in that moment that a willing heart creates a hearing ear.

Tune your heart to hear from heaven. Reach out to God with thanksgiving. When you are genuine before Him and willing to go His way, nothing will be able to stop you from receiving His best.

# *JOURNAL*

_____

_____

_____

_____

_____

_____

_____

_____

_____

_____

_____

_____

_____

_____

_____

_____

_____

_____

_____

# 45

## SAY SOMETHING

*"Blessed is she who believed, for there will be a fulfillment of those things which were told her from the Lord."*
*Luke 1:45 (NKJV)*

In Luke 1, an angel of the Lord appears and surprises a young girl named Mary, and he delivers some news to her that will change her life—and, ultimately, ours too. "Do not be afraid," he says to her, "for you have found favor with God" (v.30). He tells her that the Holy Spirit is going to come upon her and that she will conceive and bear a son that will be called the Son of the Highest, the very Son of God.

Clearly, Mary is more than a little bewildered by what Gabriel says, and she probably has many questions she wants to ask him, but her response in Luke 1:38 is evidence of why God uses this young girl in His plan to save the world. "Behold the maidservant of the Lord!" she says. "Let it be to me according to your word."

In the next few verses of Luke 1, Mary goes to visit her relative Elizabeth who is also pregnant at the time. As soon as Mary walks through the door and says hello, the baby in Elizabeth gives her a good kick; she is filled with the Holy Spirit and begins prophesying on the spot! She says many marvelous things to Mary, but I want to draw your attention to something she says found in Luke 1:45:

*"Blessed is she who believed, for there will be a fulfillment of those things, which were told her from the Lord."*

God was preparing to bless humanity on a level never seen before, but to do so, He needed someone who would simply take Him at His word, regardless of how impossible it seemed. It's hard to imagine how this whole thing would have or even could have played out if Mary had been unbelieving when she heard "the Word." But because she simply believed what she was told, the Spirit of God speaking through Elizabeth declared, "You're blessed! And because you believed that the things you heard from God are going to happen, it is guaranteed."

What is it going to take for you and me to see the improbable and do the impossible?

First, you need to hear from God. You need to make it a point to find out what He has said in His Word about you, about your life, your healing, your prosperity. Get quiet, and let Him speak to you by the same Holy Spirit that spoke to and through Elizabeth to Mary. Faith comes by hearing the Word of God, and how can you believe if you haven't heard? If you're trying to believe without having heard from God, that's called *make-believe*; it produces nothing.

Secondly, once you've heard from God, you must decide how you will respond to what He has said to you. When He presents you with a vision of your life that seems well-outside the realm of possibility, will you give voice to all your questions, concerns, doubts, and fears? Or will you, like Mary, boldly say, "Let it be to me according to your word"? How you respond will mean the difference between having what God promises or living without it. So say something already!

# JOURNAL

---

# 46

## SEEK AND FIND

*"But seek first the kingdom of God and His righteousness,*
*and all these things shall be added to you."*
*Matthew 6:33 (NKJV)*

During my last summer in college, I worked at a preschool and day camp for kids. One day, my boss came running into the office wide-eyed and thrilled over what had just happened to him, and he had to tell me the whole story. He had received a phone call from a lady in Kentucky who claimed to have information on a treasure she believed to be buried in a state park not far from where we lived.

Just a few months before this she had started reading a book with her son called *A Treasure's Trove*, an interactive story for children and adults filled with puzzles, hidden poems, and layers of clues that led to the twelve hidden creatures in the story. Every night, the mother/son team was on a search to find the hidden creatures of the book, especially since they found out that the author of the story had actually hidden twelve gold tokens in twelve state parks across the U.S. It gets even better. The author had hired a famous jeweler to create twelve corresponding elaborate jewels with a combined value of over 1 million dollars. If you could decipher the puzzles, they would lead you to a gold token that could be used to redeem the matching jewel. In other words, you could cash in big time.

The lady from Kentucky had asked my boss if he would help her find the caterpillar token that was worth $12,000. If you knew him, you'd know he was usually doing something mischievous and always up for a new adventure. This was way more intriguing than his last geocaching escapade, so he quickly agreed and took one of his friends along for the ride.

They arrived at the state park and followed her directions closely to find the tree where she thought the token was hidden. My boss spied out the park all weekend, watching as people who were also on to the treasure surrounded the area and tried to get the coin out with a magnet. But he knew it was impossible because a magnet cannot stick to gold. He waited till the treasure hunters cleared out and then decided to use a Shop-Vac from his truck to get the token out of the tree.

The one-of-a-kind gold token that he held in his hand mesmerized me, not because of what it was worth, but because of the adventure it represented. As he told me his story, I was so stirred up that I felt like it was my adventure too.

The first part of any adventure is to seek. Matthew 6:33 says, "Seek first the kingdom of God and His righteousness, and all these things shall be added unto you." We were never meant to seek the riches; they were meant to seek after us. After my boss found the gold token in the tree, the lady from Kentucky gave him half of her reward. He later said that they had never discussed splitting the earnings before he went out on the hunt. That showed me that the adventure itself meant more to him than the money.

Our motive should never be money. Instead, we should crave the King and His kingdom. If we will do His will and follow His map, there will be treasures waiting for us around every twist and every turn. His plan and His provision go hand-in-hand, and on His path, there are pleasures forevermore! But we will only find them after we discover who is most valuable in life and begin to seek a rich relationship with Him. Jesus is the ultimate Treasure. To find Him is to find life.

# *J O U R N A L*

_____

_____

_____

_____

_____

_____

_____

_____

_____

_____

_____

_____

_____

_____

_____

_____

_____

_____

_____

# 47

## YOU NEED SOME REST

*"Come to Me, all you who labor and are heavy laden, and I will give you rest." Matthew 11:28 (NKJV)*

In Matthew 11:28 Jesus said, "Come to Me, all you who labor and are heavy laden, and I will give you rest." These words from Jesus are two things: a revelation and an invitation. Every word, every action, every message, and every miracle in the life of Jesus is a revelation of the heart of His Father. When He said, "Come to Me, all you who labor and are heavy laden, and I will give you rest," He was revealing how serious God is about you and me entering into His rest for our lives. Our Father, like any good parent, could tell just by looking at us, His kids, that we were in desperate need of rest.

I probably don't have to tell you that stress levels in our country and all over the world are at all-time highs, but you and I were not created to walk according to the course of this world. There is supposed to be something different about us. And though we can't stop natural stressors from occurring in our lives, we certainly can change our responses to them and prevent them from affecting us the same way they're affecting everybody else. The key to living this way is learning to enter into the rest that Jesus has invited us into.

You will find that when you let your guard down and fail to rest by faith, that it's the little things in life that pile up and start affecting your soul the most. Things like getting the kids up and out the door on time in the mornings, or running late while you sit in traffic on the way to work. Every day-scenarios like these can be frustrating and, sadly, many people completely lose their joy before 10 o'clock in the morning because of a car that won't start, cranky kids, or bad traffic. Most of these kinds of stress instigators are naturally occurring and there's not much we can do to stop or change them. But there is something we can do to change the way they affect us.

For a brief time in our family, Sarah and the kids and I lived with my parents while we waited for the house we were moving into to become available. Their house was nearly an hour from school and work and for months we would get up early, rush to get out the door, then fight traffic, trains, and our own bad attitudes all the way to school. One day the four of us got in the car for the long drive to school just like we had for months, but instead of sitting in silence or stewing in frustration, we decided to sing. Justus started singing a song called, "Happy Day," and soon we all joined in singing, "Oh! Happy day, happy day! You washed my sins away!" For the better part of an hour we sang, praised, played air guitar and drums until we got to school. Traffic was the same that day as it had been all the days before, but instead of arriving at school already burned out, we got there laughing and singing and praising God, which set a tone of joy for the remainder of our day. Praise and worship is one of the quickest ways to enter into the rest that Jesus has offered us, and it has the power to completely change the course of your day and even your life.

# JOURNAL

_____

_____

_____

_____

_____

_____

_____

_____

_____

_____

_____

_____

_____

_____

_____

_____

_____

_____

_____

_____

_____

_____

_____

_____

_____

# 48

## POWER OFF TO POWER UP

*"Yes, a person is a fool to store up earthly wealth but not have a rich relationship with God." Luke 12:21 (NLT)*

Once, in a time of prayer, I asked the Lord to show me how to be the wife that Jeremy needs and the mommy my kids need. The Holy Spirit spoke to my heart a phrase that has helped me every day since. He said in His still, small voice, "Nurture or neglect."

Immediately I thought of a seed. After it is planted, it needs to be watered, it needs to be attended to, it needs to be nurtured in order to flourish. It needs to sit in the sun, and then it will grow. I thought about my family, the treasures God has given me. If I want them to flourish, I must nurture them, love them, pay attention to them, water them with my words, and spend time sowing all that I can into them. If I nurture them, they will grow.

On the other hand, whatever we neglect will begin to fade, waste away, and decay. I had a plant, a fiddle leaf fig, that I so enjoyed. But sometimes I would go out of town and forget to water it. Once while I was gone, a friend moved it to where it didn't get sunlight for days. When I returned, I found it with its great big leaves starting to turn brown and wither away.

There are some practical things we can do to nurture our families and cultivate rich relationships at home. You've probably noticed that we are a generation that has become addicted to our phones and other devices. Please hear my heart on this: I am not anti-phones or tablets. There have certainly been times I have gladly handed my children the iPad™ so that I was able to finish a conversation with a friend. But I do think that we should stop and identify anything in our lives that steals our time and attention from people that we are meant to love.

When I pick my kids up from school, I do my best to give my phone a break so that when they tell me all about their day, I am fully present and fully engaged. I am determined to stop wasting moments and start making memories.

It's a fact that when we turn off our phones, we talk more, we go deeper, we come closer, and our love grows for each other. Jeremy and I lived hundreds of miles apart from each other from the time we met until our wedding day! There were weeks and weeks that would pass without seeing each other in person. All we had were long-distance conversations that would many times last all the way through the night. Looking back, I can see that our relationship was being built with nothing but the words we exchanged.

I want my children to realize what is truly valuable in life, to learn early on that relationships make life rich, especially their relationships with the Lord. In Luke 12:21 (NLT), Jesus tells us that "a person is a fool to store up earthly wealth but not have a rich relationship with God." Twenty years from now, my kids won't remember mindless games they played on the tablet, but they will definitely remember the moments we spent with God and with each other.

So my challenge to you is to nurture your family. Your answer may just be to turn off the phone. Stop playing *Words With Friends*™, and have some actual words with friends. Cultivate rich relationships with God and with people. The word *cultivate* gives the impression that it may require some work: a little digging, a little plowing, and definitely some sowing. But the rewards are so worth it!

## *JOURNAL*

---

---

---

---

---

---

---

---

---

---

---

---

---

---

---

---

---

---

---

---

# 49

## DON'T BACK OFF THE VISION

*"Where there is no vision, the people perish..."*
*Proverbs 29:18 (KJV)*

I have realized that something unique happens for a small child when their father reaches down, picks them up, and holds them at his own eye level. They can see, if only for a few minutes, exactly what their father sees. As grown-ups, it's easy for us to take for granted what this sudden change of scenery must be like for little ones. One moment, everything is bigger than they are, then the next moment they are lifted above what was blocking their vision, and like Daddy, they can see ahead to what's coming.

This experience is not unlike what happens to a believer when they begin to get a glimpse of what God has called them to and created them for. Most people's lives are spent serving the demands of whatever is directly in front of them, unable to see around the giant debt, the stack of bills, or even the tall walls unknowingly built by their families, societies, or culture that exist to limit their vision. But then, in a moment of fellowship with the Father, He reaches down, picks them up to His eye level, and they can see exactly what He sees for their lives. This is what it means to have a vision from God for your life.

We know from Proverbs 29:18 that with vision, people thrive; without it, we perish. If you haven't already seen a glimpse of your future,

I assure you, it's coming. Sadly, there are Christians who know all too well what the call of God is on their lives but have chosen to ignore it and refuse to pursue it. Why would anyone choose to live without vision? Simply put - fear. The truth is, vision will always create a need. In fact, the need created by a vision from God will always be bigger than what you are able to meet today with what you've got in your wallet or bank account. Some people are striving in a futile attempt to arrive at a place in life where they have no more needs. But if you have no need, then you have no vision.

When I pick up Justus or Jessie in my arms, they are instantly able to see what I see; but because of their limited experience and understanding they don't always see how I see. Something I know to be harmless and maybe even a lot of fun, might scare them initially, only because they've never seen it or done it before. But your Father is saying to you the same thing I say to my kids: "I've got you, and there is nothing to be afraid of." If you'll continue to walk by faith in God, faith in His Word, and faith in His love, you will one day see not only what He sees but how He sees it. What seems impossible right now and tries to fill you with fear, will one day soon look like the greatest adventure you've ever had. But again, don't back off the vision, and don't be afraid of the need! The God who gave you the vision for your life is faithful to supply all your need according to His riches in glory by Christ Jesus.

# JOURNAL

_____

_____

_____

_____

_____

_____

_____

_____

_____

_____

_____

_____

_____

_____

_____

_____

_____

_____

_____

_____

_____

_____

_____

_____

_____

# 50

## THE KING'S TABLE

*"He brought me to the banqueting house, And his banner over me was love."* **Song of Solomon 2:4 (NKJV)**

A month before giving birth to each of my children, I developed symptoms of a condition called "Nesting." Many husbands view this as a serious syndrome, but to a pregnant woman, it is only a case of rushing hormones that kick in as a sign the baby is coming very soon. The only cure for the mother-to-be is to spend night and day getting the house ready.

In my case, every detail had to be just perfect for my sweet babies to arrive. From the kitchen to the nursery, it all had to be cleaned and decorated. I guess I expected each baby to be carried into our house for the first time and exclaim, "Wow Mom, what an amazing coffee table display!" I look back now and realize I may have gone a little overboard.

My favorite nesting project of all was the dining room table that I designed and had built for us. A table has always been one of the most important pieces of furniture in my house, not only because of its appearance, but because of what it represents. A table is a place where we fellowship and experience love.

Do you remember the old song, "He brought me to His banqueting table, and His banner over me is love?" It comes from a passage of scripture in Song of Solomon 2:4 that says, "He brought me to the banqueting house, and his banner over me was love." Can you imagine being invited to dine at the King's table? To be personally escorted by Him, to sit with Him, to have a one-on-one conversation with Him, and then to feast on a meal prepared by Him?

At His table there is always good conversation, good food, and a lot of laughter. It's a place where you enjoy Him and He enjoys you. Some people have a bad opinion of God, and they see Him as hard and harsh. But nothing could be further from the truth. He's not angry with you, He's enamored by you. When you walk into a room, He smiles and He looks at you with love. Because of Jesus, He will never hold your sin over your head. His banner over you is love!

Jesus loves you so much that He will never just serve you cold leftovers from someone else's plate. He's always preparing a unique menu just for you, using all the freshest and the finest ingredients, and when you taste it, you will see that He is a good cook! There is never a shortage at His table. You will find a bottomless bowl of healing that lasts a lifetime. And make sure to drink from the pitcher of provision that never runs dry. He always serves all you can eat until you are so full you have more than enough for all of your neighbors. Psalm 23:5 says, "You prepare a table before me in the presence of my enemies; You anoint my head with oil; my cup runs over."

When He invites you over for dinner, you'll never be left out or forced to sit at the kiddy table. You're royalty now, and you can be confident that He'll never leave you standing but will always require you to sit. To be seated is to be at rest in Him. To be at rest in Him is to know He is the Head of the table, Host of this party, and He will satisfy your mouth with good things! He is preparing a perfect place for you in this life on earth and working on your mansion in heaven. Apparently I'm not the only one with nesting issues!

# JOURNAL

_____

_____

_____

_____

_____

_____

_____

_____

_____

_____

_____

_____

_____

_____

_____

_____

_____

_____

_____

_____

_____

_____

_____

_____

# 51

## EXTRA! EXTRA!

*"So when they were filled, He said to His disciples, "Gather up the fragments that remain, so that nothing is lost." Therefore they gathered them up, and filled twelve baskets with the fragments of the five barley loaves which were left over by those who had eaten." John 6:12-13 (NKJV)*

More than a hundred years ago, newspaper publishers began printing what they called the "extra edition"—important or sensational news that arrived too late to go out in the normal paper. Of course, we're all familiar with the scenes played out in old movies where a young kid stands on the street corner waving a newspaper in the air shouting, "Extra! Extra! Read all about it!"

Some years ago, our family of four moved out of our home and into a new one. If you've ever packed up and moved before, then you know how much time, effort, and money goes into it. In addition to the cost of moving, there was the added expenditures for new furniture, decorations, and all the other stuff that it takes to make a new place feel warm and cozy. The first week we were there, the Lord put it strongly in my heart for our family to begin claiming *extra*. Sarah and I started encouraging each other by saying, "This is our summer of extra!" Every day for weeks we would tell each other and our kids that we would have enough to meet the needs of our new home, and we would have extra...extra to sow, extra to do what God has assigned us to do, and extra to do all that is in our heart to do.

One morning as I sat in our nearly empty living room reading my Bible, the Holy Spirit sent me to John 6. It's in this chapter that Jesus takes five loaves and two fish and then turns them into a feast that feeds more than 5,000 people. I got to verse eleven and noticed that there was enough food for all those people to eat "as much as they wanted." But the miracle didn't stop there. John 6:12-13 says, "So when they were filled, He said to His disciples, 'Gather up the fragments that remain, so that nothing is lost.' Therefore they gathered them up, and filled twelve baskets with the fragments of five barley loaves which were left over by those who had eaten." Not only did everybody get filled up and satisfied, but there were baskets and baskets of leftovers. There was *extra*!

For days after that, it seemed like every time I read my Bible, I was seeing in it God's nature, ability, and willingness to provide more than enough for His people. I began walking around the house waving my Bible in the air saying, "Extra! Extra! Read all about it!"

And do you know what happened just a few days after we started claiming extra? Extra started coming in by the hundreds and thousands! I suggest that you and your family start saying the same thing ours did. Begin right now to say that you are in a season of extra and that there will be enough to fill you up with extra to sow, extra to fulfill your assignment, and extra to do all that is on your heart to do! Take some *extra* time to set your eyes and ears on God's Word to specifically build your faith for extra. You must let your heart enlarge, and your capacity to receive must get bigger, because if He can't get it in your heart, then He can't get it in your hands.

# JOURNAL

_____

_____

_____

_____

_____

_____

_____

_____

_____

_____

_____

_____

_____

_____

_____

_____

_____

_____

_____

_____

_____

_____

_____

_____

_____

_____

_____

_____

_____

_____

# 52

## TASTE AND SEE

*"Oh, taste and see that the Lord is good; Blessed is the man who trusts in Him!" Psalm 34:8 (NKJV)*

I've always been somewhat of a foodie. I like food and look forward to a good meal with my family. Some of my favorite memories are at the dinner table with people that I love, especially those long meals where we laugh and cry together, tell stories, eat delicious food, and talk about the goodness of God.

To this day, my grandparents still laugh when they tell the story of how I used to bless the food as a little girl. They said I would bow my head and close my eyes to pray, and then I would begin to thank the Lord for every single item on the table. I was just so hungry and excited that I didn't want to forget about anything on my plate. You can imagine this took forever, so halfway through the prayer, I would open one eye just enough to make sure I remembered every side and every condiment. "Lord, thank You for the turkey and the green beans and the sweet-potato casserole, and those rolls, and that butter . . . ." One time I stopped in the middle of the prayer and exclaimed, "Ew! What's that?"

Spiritual food is just as real and important as natural food. If you want to be nourished and healthy, you must eat it every single day. It's always better to start eating again before you feel like you're starving, but if you're hungry, just keep on feeding, and you will get full. Just as natural food brings energy to keep the body going, spiritual food is the fuel for your future.

The Word of God is our spiritual food, and it is delicious. Jeremiah 15:16 (KJV) says, " Thy words were found, and I did eat them; and thy word was unto me the joy and rejoicing of mine heart." *The Message* translation reads, "When your words showed up, I ate them—swallowed them whole. What a feast!"

If you always fill up on junk food, you won't have room for anything good. But if you eat all the greens and veggies and fruits that you're supposed to in a day, you won't desire the bad stuff. Listening to teaching that doesn't bring you abundant life is like taking in empty calories. Check the label on your food! Is it full of additives and preservatives that will entertain your soul but leave you weak? Or is it real and raw and able to build you up and make you strong? Ingesting words of faith and victory is like eating fine food. The quality of the word that you eat will determine the quality of life that you live.

How you eat is just as important as what you eat. Doctors have found that eating on the go is not the best for your health. One of my least favorite things to do is to rush through a good meal without taking time to savor it. Psalm 34:8 says, "Oh, taste and see that the Lord is good." To taste means to savor or to enjoy completely. We shouldn't rush through our time with the Lord like driving through a fast-food restaurant. He is not to be endured; He is to be enjoyed. Take time to slow down and savor His goodness.

Find out from the Word everything that He has set before you, and then close your eyes and start thanking Him for every item on your plate.

# JOURNAL

_____

_____

_____

_____

_____

_____

_____

_____

_____

_____

_____

_____

_____

_____

_____

_____

_____

_____

_____

_____

_____

_____

_____

_____

_____

# SALVATION PRAYER

God is a loving Father who knows you better than you know yourself. Now He wants you to know Him in the same personal way. The first and most important step in this is to make Jesus first place in your life. Just pray this simple prayer aloud:

*Heavenly Father, I am coming to You now in the Name of Your Son Jesus. I believe with all my heart that He is the Savior of the world. I believe He lived, died, and rose from the dead, and that He did it all for me. I ask You to cleanse me of all my sin. Wash me clean and make me new. Thank You for the gift that You gave me in Jesus. I receive Him now as my Lord. Fill me with Your Holy Spirit. I receive His help, courage, and strength to live a victorious life. I am Yours forever. In Jesus' Name. Amen.*

# WAYS TO GET
# THE WORD

———

**+**

## THE LEGACY STUDIOS APP

*Available on iOS & Android*

**+**

## PEARSONSMINISTRIES.COM

*Watch LegacyTV, music videos, free sermons, and more*

**+**

## LEGACYTV

*For local stations & times, visit pearsonsministries.com*

**+**

## PEARSONS MINISTRIES PODCASTS

**+**

## THE LEGACY LETTER

# LEGACY CHURCH

*GREEN MOUNTAIN FALLS | COLORADO*

*www.legacychurch.family*

# LEGACY TV

WITH **JEREMY & SARAH PEARSONS**

# THE LEGACY LETTER

*A Pearsons Ministries Intl Publication*

*For more information about LegacyTV and to subscribe to The Legacy Letter, visit us online at pearsonsministries.com*

# WORSHIP MUSIC
*by Sarah Pearsons*

## LOVE SONGS FOR THE KING
*The debut worship project from Sarah Pearsons. This CD features 12 original songs that will ignite the heart of worship within you.*

## STRENGTH & BEAUTY IN THE PRESENCE OF THE HEALER
*A collection of songs lifted from the pages of Scripture. This peaceful compilation focuses on ministering healing to the body and rest to the soul.*

## IN LIGHT OF LOVE & GRACE
*The latest album from Sarah Pearsons, featuring 10 original songs.*

***Worship music by Sarah Pearsons available on iTunes***